Samuel Beckett's Novel Watt

Gottfried Büttner

Foreword by Deirdre Bair
Translated by Joseph P. Dolan

University of Pennsylvania Press
Philadelphia

For Marie Renate

Credits

All quotations from Samuel Beckett's novel Watt *are reprinted courtesy of Grove Press, Inc., 196 West Houston Street, New York, NY 10014.*

Photographs in this volume are by the author.

Translated from the German, Samuel Becketts Roman "Watt": Eine Untersuchung des gnoseologischen Grundzuges *by Gottfried Büttner. Copyright © 1981 by Carl Winter Universitätsverlag, Heidelberg.*

Library of Congress Cataloging in Publication Data

Büttner, Gottfried, 1926–
    Samuel Beckett's novel Watt.

    Translation of: Samuel Becketts Roman "Watt."
    Bibliography: p.
    Includes index.
    1. Beckett, Samuel, 1906–   . Watt. I. Title.
PR6003.E282W343213   1985   823'.912   84-7234
ISBN 0–8122–7932–8

Printed in the United States of America

Contents

Acknowledgments

I wish to express my gratitude to those who have been most intimately involved in the production of the American edition of my book on Samuel Beckett's novel *Watt*.

Professor Deirdre Bair, an expert of great renown on Samuel Beckett, has been a source of constant help; her introduction serves as a fitting beginning for the book. Mr. Joseph P. Dolan deserves many thanks for his thorough translation. I am also grateful to Professors G. Rohmann, K. Schoell, and Chr. W. Thomsen, who encouraged my study in Germany.

Mr. Maurice English, late Director of the University of Pennsylvania Press, bravely committed himself to the publication of this book; I am saddened that he could not live to see it finished. To him, and to Ingalill Hjelm and Catherine Gjerdingen for their skillful editorial work, my sincere thanks.

Introduction

It has its place . . . as will perhaps appear in time.
Samuel Beckett's Watt

For many years, Samuel Beckett's novel *Watt* has either been overlooked or explained away in the most cursory fashion by scholars and critics who have otherwise paid the most scrupulous attention to the rest of his canon.

Watt is indeed a curious novel, one which baffles and perplexes as it subjects the reader to a progression of dazzling fictional enigmas. The sense of textual displacement it conveys culminates in an addenda of such force that the sternness of its admonition is as dismaying as it is puzzling.

Beckett wrote the novel *Watt* following the more accessible *Murphy*, but it was not published until nine years later, thus perhaps heightening the sense of displacement, of something perhaps askew. Beckett had already become famous for *Waiting for Godot* and the trilogy, *Molloy, Malone Dies*, and *The Unnamable*, when a group of young writers he called the "*Merlin* juveniles" published *Watt* in their magazine.

From the beginning of his career as a writer, Beckett has always viewed his works as part of a series, with each work having its rightful place. This probably adds to the equivocation he expressed toward *Watt* during the years before it was published. In a letter to the late George Reavey, the Irish poet who sometimes acted as Beckett's literary agent during the early years of his career, Beckett described *Watt* in a manner that is at the same time both offhanded and caring: "It is an unsatisfactory book, written in dribs and drabs, first on the run, then of an evening after the clod-hopping, during the occupation, but it has its place in the series, as will perhaps appear in time."[1] And, a little later, when Reavey was unsuccessful in finding a publisher to accept *Watt*, Beckett wrote, somewhat in the same vein, "He is a nice fellow, but his word is certainly without importance."[2]

It was with relief then that Beckett wrote to Reavey six years later to tell him that "our old misery, *Watt*,"[3] was about to be published in *Merlin*.

Beckett's equivocal attitude to *Watt* can be seen in one final extract from his correspondence, this time in a letter to Dr. Gottfried Büttner, who was then writing this book: "I think *Watt* was begun in Paris in 1942, then continued evenings mostly in Roussillon and finished 1945 in Dublin and Paris. It was written as it came, without preestablished plan. I have not looked at it since translating it with Ludovic and Agnes Janvier many years ago and so am hardly qualified to answer your questions of detail."[4]

Dr. Gottfried Büttner (b. 1926 in Dresden), studied medicine at the Universities of Göttingen and Tübingen. Earlier, he had been educated in a Waldorf school where he became interested in the teachings of Rudolf Steiner. He became a member of the Anthroposophical Society in 1947 when he was twenty-one, and has continued his study of anthroposophy ever since. His medical work is strongly influenced by it, as are his literary interpretations.

Dr. Büttner, who is a Doctor of Philosophy as well as a physician, became interested in Beckett's writings in the 1960s when he saw German language productions of Beckett's plays in his home town, Kassel. He was so struck by a production of *Krapp's Last Tape* in particular that he sent a letter to Beckett in care of his German publisher. Beckett replied, expressing gratitude and pleasure in Dr. Büttner's response to the play. He also mentioned that he had many fond memories of Kassel, where he had visited his aunt and uncle, Mr. and Mrs. William Sinclair, at the end of the 1920s and the beginning of the 1930s.

There was no further correspondence until three years later, on the occasion of Beckett's sixtieth birthday, when Dr. Büttner sent greetings and Beckett replied. The correspondence led to their friendship and intensified Dr. Büttner's subsequent literary study of Beckett's writing. Since that time, Dr. Büttner and his wife, Dr. Marie Renate Büttner (she is also a physician in joint practice with her husband), have met Beckett more than half a dozen times. These meetings have taken place in Germany, mainly in Berlin, when Beckett was there in connection with theatrical and television productions, in Paris, and in Ussy, where Beckett keeps a country home.

Dr. Büttner first learned of the existence of *Watt* in April 1969 when he visited Beckett in Ussy. Beckett spoke of having worked for the previous two years on its German translation. While Elmar Tophoven, the excellent translator of Beckett's other writings into German, and his wife, Erika, also a translator, had prepared the *Rohentwurf*, or first draft, Beckett had done the arduous work of refining the text for publication.[5]

This was the genesis of Dr. Büttner's interest in *Watt*, and for the next ten to fifteen years, as he began this book and wrote others, there was correspondence between him and Beckett which touched occasionally upon translation, philological intention, and interpretation of the text. Beckett, as he has always done in the past, and as Dr. Büttner has stated in this book, made it very clear that he would not explicate his writings and would continue his insistence that they stand as separate entities. However, the degree of interest that Beckett has shown in Dr. Büttner's examination of *Watt* is without parallel, and so one can state with confidence that the arguments which Dr. Büttner states as his own do indeed reflect Beckett's as well. When the German edition of Dr. Büttner's study was published in 1981, Beckett sent Dr. Büttner the manuscript of his most recent dramatic writing, *Quad*, in appreciation of it.

Dr. Büttner's earlier book, *Absurdes Theater und Bewusstseinswandel* (dedicated to Samuel Beckett),[6] is a study of the plays of Beckett and of Eugène Ionesco. In this book, Dr. Büttner deals with the "change of consciousness" which expresses itself in the so-called "absurd character of the plays," so that a "kind of soul realism" leads to a better understanding of "spiritual facts."[7] Dr. Büttner's interest in depicting reality, or in what he calls the "subject-object" relationship, is one which has fascinated him since he studied literature as a student, and which informs and influences both that book and the present study.

In the chapter on Beckett's plays in the earlier book, Dr. Büttner used the word "epistemological" to approximate the original German *erkenntnistheoretisch*, but Beckett suggested that a better translation, one closer to the original, would be the word "gnosiological." Thus, the term by which the present study was titled in the original German was suggested by Beckett as most closely describing what it is that he has intended his writing to represent.

In a letter to me, Dr. Büttner explained the selection of the word "gnosiological" and its attendant meaning in the context of Beckett's writing. In a conversation about his plays, Beckett told Dr. Büttner that *Endgame* was "better visualized" than *Waiting for Godot*, which, Dr. Büttner writes,

> shows the way he looks at his undertakings. Beckett, as you know, sees things from the deep within him, whilst, as he once said to me, James Joyce saw everything from far away (being in command of a brilliant memory, as Beckett added). I understand this as a very fundamental characterization of their different points of view, Joyce being a distant observer, Beckett deeply involved in existential problems, searching with a torch in the dark. Joyce, Beckett said, saw everything from a "far cosmic distance," which points to his intellectual attitude and objectivity toward the subjects of his writing.
>
> In my opinion, Beckett's "research" is in a quite different way "objective," i.e. mentally realistic. Although he is deeply involved in problems he discovers within himself (mirroring the world of objects around him and spiritual "facts" such as philosophical questions), he arrives at a stage equally "realistic," (or shall I call it "eternal"?) . . . [as] Joyce in a quite different way. Behind this lies the basic question of what is REALITY and how we can discover or perceive it. In my opinion, both great writers are realists, but on different levels of existence, if realism is taken as in German, *Wirklichkeit* or *wirklichkeitsgemäss*, and not as a category of literature.[8]

Thus, one can understand Dr. Büttner's interest in the level of inner reality which the description of "Watt's world of words" can lead one to postulate. In this book, Dr. Büttner raises the question of whether or not a novel such as *Watt* "legitimately enlarges man's knowledge beyond the generally accepted (and otherwise dogmatized) borders of our consciousness."[9] Dr. Büttner's view holds that because so many of Beckett's characters are first met when they are mired in hopeless situations, on the fringe of existence, or on or beyond the threshold of death, the reader is subjected to an unexperienced level of reality. Having penetrated this realm, Beckett, looking on from his own mental sphere, exploring the limits of the reader's existence, thus enlarges the reader's knowledge.

Rather than heeding Beckett's admonition, "no symbols where none intended," and regarding it as an absolute prohibition, Dr. Büttner chooses instead to consider it as a warning for the overly eager application of personal symbolism and analogy, as "Beckett's warning for those who lightheartedly employ too much of their own imagination in interpreting the actual text."[10]

Dr. Büttner, in this study, interprets *Watt* through hermeneutic analysis in order to demonstrate the metaconscious state of being which he believes is central not only to this novel but also to Beckett's entire *oeuvre*. Dr. Büttner believes that the writing of Rudolf Steiner contains much that is applicable to Beckett, particularly in the curiously similar way in which Steiner's spiritual phenomena parallel "Watt's world of words," and he concludes with a discussion of current research into the physiology of sense perception, which is in keeping with his interest in the psychological and spiritual content of contemporary literature.

Perhaps the statement of Professor Gerd Rohmann in the foreword to the German edition of this book describes it best: "Dr. Büttner has never been content with the spiritual positivism of traditional medicine and has always inquired after the spiritual reality of man."

Those who read this enlightening book will agree with

Professor Rohmann that "a physician who is also a student of
literature may well have something valuable to say about these
matters."

Philadelphia   DEIRDRE BAIR
November 10, 1983

Notes

1. Samuel Beckett to George Reavey, May 14, 1947.
2. Samuel Beckett to George Reavey, June 25, 1947.
3. Samuel Beckett to George Reavey, May 12, 1953.
4. Samuel Beckett to Dr. Gottfried Büttner, December 4, 1978.
By mentioning only the Janviers, Beckett seems to have forgotten
that he spent more than two years working to perfect the German
translation prepared by Elmar and Erika Tophoven during the late
1960s.
5. Before the Büttners could read the German text of *Watt*,
they received a copy in English from the author himself. Beckett's
inscription reads: "for Gottfried and Marie Renate Büttner from Samuel Beckett with all good wishes, Paris, July 1969." Beckett sent the
British edition of *Watt* (John Calder, 1963) to Dr. Büttner's second
home in Southern France.
6. *Absurdes Theater und Bewusstseinswandel,* Westliche Berliner
Verlagsgesellschaft, Heenemann KG, 1968.
7. Dr. Gottfried Büttner to Deirdre Bair, April 29, 1982.
8. Ibid.
9. *English and American Studies in German: Summaries of Theses
and Monographs, A Supplement to* Anglia (Tübingen: Max Niemeyer
Verlag, 1981), pp. 105–6.
10. Ibid.

In Search of a Hidden Meaning: An Introduction

There is a certain esoteric quality hidden skeletally in Beckett's work.
    A. J. Leventhal[1]

I

---

1. "The Beckett Hero," in *Samuel Beckett: A Collection of Critical Essays*, ed. Martin Esslin (Englewood Cliffs, N.J., 1965), p. 48. Leventhal was a professor at Beckett's former university, Trinity College in Dublin, and later lived in Paris until his death. He and Beckett were friends for many years.

Problems of Interpretation

The value of a novel as a form of knowledge is of interest to both the literary critic and the anthropologist. An epistemological interpretation serves the purpose of defining the content of a work of literature. This is the goal of the essay on Samuel Beckett's novel *Watt* presented here.

This study thus deals with the underlying gnosiological aspect of Beckett's novel. Other authors have approached *Watt* in the spirit of literary criticism or have studied its effects on other writers. This essay, however, approaches it from the twin viewpoints of an anthropologically oriented phenomenology and psychology.

All interpretations depend on the standpoint of the interpreter. This relativizes the value of such studies, which must therefore abandon any claim to exclusiveness. This limitation does not, however, render an attempt at interpretation such as the present one superfluous. The observer must in a certain sense become what he observes, because subject and object are qualitatively equivalent in a novel such as *Watt*, which is fundamentally an examination of consciousness.

An encounter with Beckett's works almost necessarily results in a need to interpret. It is apparent that Beckett desires, even demands, interpretation, in spite of several defensive remarks of his to the contrary. For example, he has often been asked whom he intended Godot to represent and what the character means. He has either dismissed such questions by saying he once knew someone with the name Godeau, or, as Alan Schneider reports, has answered, "If I knew, I would have said so in the play."[2] This shows that Beckett is an artist with no interest in providing commentary on himself or in

2. "Waiting for Beckett," *Chelsea Review,* no. 2 (1958): pp. 3–20; reprinted in *Beckett at 60: A Festschrift* (London, 1967), p. 38. Here it is stated again: "Sam (Beckett) was perfectly willing to answer any questions of specific meaning or reference but would not—as always—go into matters of larger or symbolic meanings, preferring his work to speak for itself and letting the supposed 'meanings' fall where they may."

interpreting his own works. It is sufficient for him to formulate as precisely as possible the issues and problems he wants to present.

On the occasion of a production of *Endgame*, staged by Beckett himself at the Schiller Theater Workshop in Berlin in 1967, Beckett had the following handwritten statement reproduced in the program: "*Endgame* does not want to be anything but a mere play. Nothing less. No thought, therefore, as to riddles, solutions. For such serious stuff we have universities, churches, coffee houses, etc."[3]

With this statement, Beckett opposes the tendency, often taken to disastrous extremes in Germany, to indulge in speculative interpretation. At the same time, he contradicts

3. Program no. 187 of the Schiller Theater Workshop, 1967/68. Beckett's original German reads: "*Endspiel* will blosses Spiel sein. Nichts weniger. Von Rätseln, von Lösungen, also kein Gedanke. Es gibt für solches ernstes Zeug Universitäten, Kirchen, Cafés du Commerce u.s.w."

This statement was in response to two questions: (1) When *Endgame* was produced for the first time ten years ago, the play provoked a feeling of perplexity in most of the audience. It was felt that the author was asking riddles to which he himself did not have answers. Do you believe that *Endgame* poses riddles to the audience? (2) Are you of the opinion that the author must have a ready solution to these riddles?

Beckett answered the first question as quoted above, but it is striking that he uses the phrase "nothing less" in reference to the play, rather than "nothing more" as we might have expected. This suggests the status he wishes to grant a play or work of art. The remark that there are universities, churches, and coffee houses to provide possible answers to the riddles ("such serious stuff" as he so casually puts it) merely confirms what Alan Schneider observed as early as 1958 (see n. 2). For this reason the answer to the second question is also just as laconic: "Not the author of this play." ("Der dieses Spieles nicht." Both the questions and Beckett's answers were originally in German.)

This statement of Beckett's has been quoted frequently. It is cited, for example, in Hartmut Engelhardt and Dieter Mettler, eds., *Materialien zu Becketts Endspiel* (Frankfurt am Main, 1976), p. 6; and in Wolfgang Iser, *Die Artistik des Misslingens* (Heidelberg, 1979). In both cases the quotation is incorrect, the German version being equivalent to "*Endgame* is . . . ," instead of "wants to be." (See the facsimile of Beckett's statement reproduced in Program no. 187 of the Schiller Theater.)

himself jokingly, admitting that universities, and so forth, will inevitably devote themselves to an intellectual analysis of his works. As a second remark in this connection clearly reveals (see n. 3), he does not consider it *his* responsibility to provide answers to questions raised by his work. He has no pat answers.

Perplexity as a result of deep irritation is the response of most people confronted with Beckett's works. A compulsion to ask questions arises, not only because no answers are provided but because it seems impossible to find any valid ones. Here we find the real source of the need to interpret. This interpretive urge is felt not only by those who read Beckett, however. Because of the difficulty of these texts, they reach only a small circle of readers, who are usually eager to impose an interpretation on a text, even where none is called for. In addition, perplexity is the normal experience of the much larger group of people that sees his plays. There is also an element of intellectual seduction in Beckett's work, to which professional critics invariably submit much more easily than ordinary theatergoers. This was the case particularly at the time of the first production of major works such as *Waiting for Godot* and *Endgame,* and this was apparently the motive behind Beckett's comments quoted above on the occasion of the new Berlin production.

The irritating or provocative aspect inherent in Beckett's texts, which subsequently "discharges" in a need to interpret, has long been recognized by critics and has been accurately described by Wolfgang Iser, for example, in connection with theories of public and critical response to Beckett's works.[4]

4. Cf. Iser, *The Implicit Reader* (Baltimore and London, 1974), p. 271: "If the play won't tell him what it means, then he will decide for himself what it ought to mean. The result is that the spectator is, so to speak, dragged along in the wake of the play, trying increasingly hard to catch up by means of interpretation." The peculiar kind of mental response expressed as the "compulsion to interpret" is derived by Iser from the continuous series of negations in Beckett's texts. Iser presented a paper on this in Berlin in 1973, which is published in *Das Werk von Samuel Beckett: Berliner Colloquium,* ed. Hans

Some biographical information, which I can supply on the basis of my own experiences with, and knowledge of, the author Samuel Beckett, will be used in support of my interpretation. I am aware that Beckett tries to retreat behind his texts. John Pilling probably chose the following epigraph for his book *Samuel Beckett* for this very reason: "The author is never interesting."[5] This statement of Beckett's does indeed characterize the relationship he seeks between himself and his work. At the same time, there are definite biographical connections between any author and a fictional work of art: "The most obvious origin of a work of art is its creator, the author; and hence an explanation in terms of the personality and the life of the writer has been one of the oldest and best established methods of literary study."[6]

In the present study, a careful analysis of the text has priority, although information which could be assembled from sources other than the text (e.g., letters and conversations) cannot be ignored. These biographical details can illuminate and buttress an interpretation. My argumentation, however, does not rely on this information, but rather on hermeneutic logic.

The Genesis of the Novel Watt

Beckett wrote *Watt* during World War II. In a letter dated April 12, 1978, he wrote, "*Watt* was begun in Paris 1942, then continued evenings mostly in Roussillon and finished 1945 in Dublin & Paris."[7] He had found a haven from the German army of occupation in the Département of Vaucluse and was

---

Mayer and Uwe Johnson (Frankfurt am Main, 1975), pp. 54ff. See also Wolfgang Iser, *The Act of Reading: A Theory of Aesthetic Response* (Baltimore and London, 1978); and Manfred Smuda, *Becketts Prosa als Metasprache* (Munich, 1970).

5. (London and Boston, 1976), p. 1.

6. Rene Wellek and Austin Warren, *Theory of Literature*, 3d ed. (New York, 1956), p. 75.

7. The recipient of this and all following letters is the present author.

forced to work on the land in exchange for food during this period. Deirdre Bair, in her biography of Beckett, cites a letter which Beckett wrote to his friend George Reavey on May 14, 1947, concerning the genesis of the novel *Watt*.[8] Here he writes that he composed the book in "dribs and drabs, first on the run, then of an evening after the clod-hopping." *Watt* was thus written during an extremely difficult period for the author.

The novel appeared first in installments in the Anglo-American literary journal *Merlin* between 1950 and 1953, after Reavey had tried in vain to find a publisher for it. Then, in 1953, a limited edition appeared in the Olympia Press of Paris, as volume 1 of the "Collection Merlin." The first regular edition of *Watt* was also brought out by Olympia Press, but not until 1958. The edition I have used was published by John Calder, Ltd. in 1963, and corresponds to the first edition.*

In reply to my question about the manner in which *Watt* was written, Beckett answered in the same letter of April 12, 1978, cited above, "It was written as it came, without pre-established plan." This is significant with regard to the supposition that the various chapters were not written down in the order in which they appear in the final book. In volume 2 of the Suhrkamp edition of Beckett's works, the editors, Elmar Tophoven and Klaus Birkenhauer, discuss this point and believe there are indications that, in accordance with Beckett's suggestion at the beginning of part IV of *Watt*, the novel could not have been written continuously in the sequence of chapters we now have. The question of the sequence of chapters has other aspects, however, to which I will return in chapter 3 of this study. According to Beckett's statement quoted above, there is no support for interpreting the comment at the beginning of part IV of *Watt* as bearing on the creation of the novel, as the editors of the Suhrkamp edition believe. The

8. *Samuel Beckett: A Biography* (New York and London, 1978), p. 364.

*Editor's note: Although Dr. Büttner's original study used the John Calder edition, references to *Watt* in the present translation are to the 1959 Grove Press edition.

editors emphasize, however, that one must be cautious with suppositions of this kind, "because the narrators of Beckett's novels, who so readily contradict themselves and take back their own words, cannot be believed, unless what they say can be verified elsewhere in the text."[9]

Watt was written between the novel *Murphy*, published in 1938, a book which went unrecognized in its time, and the later works *Mercier and Camier* (written in 1946–47 but not released by Beckett for publication until 1970) and the trilogy *Molloy, Malone Dies,* and *The Unnamable*, written in 1947–50. *Watt* was originally written in English, whereas the novels following it were written in French. Only much later was *Watt* translated into German by Elmar Tophoven and published by Suhrkamp in 1970. For some Beckett readers, who knew *Murphy* and the trilogy, *Watt* was like a "missing link."

Beckett himself thought of *Watt* as a successor to *Murphy*. Deirdre Bair writes in this regard, "Beckett . . . wanted readers to think of *Watt* as the continuation of a series" (p. 364). Beckett wrote to his friend George Reavey that *Watt* "has its place in the series as will perhaps appear in time."[10]

Watt is no easier to read than the trilogy, and it is striking that there is much less secondary literature on it than on Beckett's other books, quite aside from the sea of ink devoted to *Waiting for Godot*. *Watt*, in its multidimensionality, seems to be difficult to understand.

Secondary Literature on Watt

In order to provide a survey of the existing secondary literature on *Watt* without interrupting the chronology of publication,[11] the following grouping has been made: studies by

9. *Suhrkamp Werke*, ed. Elmar Tophoven and Klaus Birkenhauer (Frankfurt am Main, 1976), pp. 618–19.

10. Cited in Bair, *Samuel Beckett*, p. 364.

11. See Jackson R. Bryer, "Samuel Beckett: A Checklist of Criticism," in *Samuel Beckett Now: Critical Approaches to His Novels, Poetry, and Plays*, ed. Melvin J. Friedman (Chicago, 1970), and the bibliography at the end of this study.

authors dealing exclusively with *Watt* are discussed in the section below. This is followed by a discussion of sections or chapters of books that deal with *Watt* as part of a general consideration of Beckett's novels. Some of the secondary literature is also used in chapter 4 in order to develop my own view of *Watt* through a critical discussion of other authors.

CRITICAL STUDIES OF *WATT*

Probably the earliest study specifically on *Watt* is by Jacqueline Hoefer (1959). Her study was reprinted in 1965 in the anthology edited by Martin Esslin, *Samuel Beckett: A Collection of Critical Essays*.[12] Hoefer deals primarily with the logical aspects of the novel. At first, she observes, "Watt professes to be interested only in external, sensory phenomena . . . his approach is scientific" (p. 63). But Watt discovers quickly that this doesn't work in Mr. Knott's house: "Gradually, Watt is obliged to recognize that a description of the outer meaning in the manner practiced by scientific observers, or advocated by logical positivists, will not suffice at Mr. Knott's house" (p. 65). She concludes that here the author demonstrates the failure of any search for *reality*. Using the story of the ladder, which Beckett has Arsene, Watt's predecessor in the novel, recount, Hoefer draws comparisons to Wittgenstein's *Tractatus*, which also uses the image of a ladder which must be cast away as soon as it has been climbed. Wittgenstein, however, firmly believes that one should say nothing about which nothing can be said. It is clear that Beckett is not of the same opinion. Furthermore, Beckett was not acquainted with Wittgenstein's work at the time he wrote *Watt*. In Hoefer's essay, Watt is treated as a tragicomic figure who learns that "the irrational cannot be reached with rational tools." No one can argue with that. It is doubtful, however, that this justifies

12. See n. 1. The page numbers given in connection with the following quotations by Hoefer refer to the reprint in Esslin's anthology, *Samuel Beckett: A Collection of Critical Essays* (Englewood Cliffs, N.J., 1965), rather than to the original article, "*Watt*," in *Perspective* 11 (1959):166–82.

the conclusion of her study, namely, that Watt "ends dum, num, blin [*sic!*]" (p. 76).

David H. Hesla wrote on *Watt* in 1963 and again in 1971. His first study is entitled "The Shape of Chaos: A Reading of Beckett's *Watt*."[13] Because it deals with formal aspects of the novel, it is of secondary importance to the interpretation presented here. Hesla begins with Beckett's assertion that modern man's life is a "mess"—that is, characterized by confusion and chaos—and that, nevertheless, "every writer, as artist, has an obligation to form" (p. 85). This points to the fundamental difficulty confronting Beckett as a modern writer. He therefore quotes Beckett himself: "To find a form that accommodates this mess, that is the task of the artist now" (p. 86). Hesla considers it obvious that *Watt* is the story of a madman. The novel begins traditionally: "*Watt* is told from a point of view which seems at first to be omniscient. Then, about halfway through the work, we learn that the narrator is Watt's friend, and everything he knows about Watt has been told him by Watt himself. Only at the beginning of the third chapter do we discover that the narrator is named Sam, and that he and Watt are inmates at the same mental institution" (pp. 86–87).

Hesla also finds parallels in *Watt* to Dante's journey through hell and to the Way of the Cross, but these are quickly dropped (pp. 88–89). He makes the noteworthy comment, "Every major character, every major scene and incident, seems to invite interpretation, whether plausible or not, based on esoteric intelligence" (pp. 89–90). The study then deals with the various "stories" which are told in *Watt* and with the characteristics of Mr. Knott: "Mr. Knott may be interpreted to be in some sense an ikon of the divine" (p. 98). In this connection, Hesla discusses quotations from the Bible and finds that "we may reasonably conclude that *Watt* is the narrative of the Passion of one of the two thieves—and most likely of the one to whom the words of promise were not spoken" (p. 99).

13. *Critique* 6 (Minneapolis, 1963):85–105.

But Hesla himself recognizes the difficulties of this kind of interpretation: "The chief danger of this interpretation of the novel as an allegory in the traditional sense [is that] . . . there is far too much in the novel which cannot be accounted for by reference to a neat allegorical system" (pp. 101–2).

Hesla then turns to the structure of the work again and remarks that each section of the novel returns to the starting point in a wavelike movement. That "each of the chapters returns the reader to more or less the same world it carried him from" is an observation that every reader can verify. Whether it is correct to say that *Watt* is a book about "nothing" should be analyzed in greater detail than Hesla does here, especially since the author identifies Knott with nought: "Ultimately it makes no difference whether Mr. Knott is God or whether he is Nought; for even if he is God, he is so unavailable to the need, aspiration, and method of Watt that he might as well be not as be" (p. 105).

In his second study devoted to *Watt*,[14] Hesla discusses the failure of Watt as a truth-seeker. His starting point is that Watt is hardly capable of understanding his experiences. To this extent he differs also from Murphy. Hesla believes "the novel is a tale told by a psychotic to a psychotic and then retold to us." It is all the more remarkable, therefore, that he draws references to many thinkers who pondered problems similar to those of interest to Beckett, from the ancient Greeks (Empedocles, Democritus, etc.) to Kierkegaard, with special emphasis on Berkeley, Leibnitz, Spinoza, and Descartes (p. 73). The whole process again ends in the collapse of reason (p. 79). Hesla relativizes Mr. Knott's earlier identification with God or nought in that he compares him to the philosophers and ultimately exposes his parodistic character: "We have dressed Mr. Knott pretty heavily in the robes of symbolism though not, I hope, without justification. As a symbol of the God of parody [and he adds] but as an image of the God

---

14. David H. Hesla, *The Shape of Chaos: An Interpretation of the Art of Samuel Beckett* (Minneapolis, 1971), pp. 59–85.

of religion he is not. Instead, he is the object of yearning and love" (p. 83).

There are three studies by Ruby Cohn on *Watt* (1961, 1962, and 1964).[15] These were published either before or between the two by Hesla just discussed. The article published in 1964 is particularly easy to connect with Hesla's interpretation. Cohn's first study is purely comparative, that is, it considers *Watt* in relation to Kafka's *The Castle*. Although there are parallels here, nothing of consequence for the present interpretation can be drawn from such a comparison. *The Castle*, a novel written in 1922, describes the most extreme isolation in which a human being can find himself—an experience at the boundary of what is human. This sense of being lost is reminiscent of Beckett. The anxiety and feeling of guilt which are dominant in Kafka are not present in Beckett, however, or at least are forced far into the background by a tough power of perseverance which can be explained only by the stoicism natural to Beckett—quite aside from the fact that Kafka was a conventional storyteller in terms of form, even when he observes reality from inside as though with a "mental periscope." Beckett adopts a similar internal standpoint; that is, he turns away from external reality which has become unreliable for him. But he goes beyond Kafka in the soberness of his vision, and above all he breaks through the temporal restrictions of linear narrative structure. In *Watt*, Beckett treats phenomena which did not exist for Kafka.

Ruby Cohn's second study, *Samuel Beckett: The Comic Gamut* (1962), discusses the comic aspects of Beckett's work. It is obviously less important to the gnosiological aspect of *Watt* than her third article, which goes into philosophical aspects and is thus directly related to Hesla's interpretation. Cohn also starts with the "mess" which Beckett finds and

15. (1) "*Watt* in the Light of *The Castle*," *Comparative Literature* 13 (1961):154–66; (2) *Samuel Beckett: The Comic Gamut* (New Brunswick, N.J., 1962); and (3) "Philosophical Fragments in the Works of Samuel Beckett," *Criticism: A Quarterly for Literature and the Arts* 6 (1964):33–43; reprinted in Esslin, *Samuel Beckett*, pp. 169ff.

describes in life. Cohn and Hesla both draw attention to a corresponding statement of Beckett's, which Tom F. Driver has recorded.[16]

First, Cohn refers to the philosophical currents dominant today, namely, logical positivism and existentialism, each of which in its own way attempts to overcome the dualism of Descartes. It is assumed that Watt behaves as an ideal student of Wittgenstein, "using his senses, logic, and language with maddening meticulousness" (p. 175). Confronted with Mr. Knott's irrational existence, however, Watt's understanding breaks down: "His speech grows incoherent, and his mind breaks down, so that he has to be institutionalized" (p. 175).

The conclusion to be drawn from this, says the author, is that Watt's rationalism and empiricism lead to a form of solipsism, which is to be termed "insane." Cohn observes, "When Beckett turned from English to French as a writing language, his protagonists turned from a kind of Logical Positivism to a kind of Existentialism."

All studies of *Watt* mentioned up to now emphasize that the movement of the chief character from a rational world of thought to an irrational reality is associated with the loss of reason. Watt is insane, and he tells stories that are more or less insane, which therefore have no logical coherence to a "friend" (fellow inmate) in a mental hospital. It is assumed that Beckett is describing the end of all logical understanding.

In the winter of 1962-63, an article by J. Mitchell Morse on the contemplative side of Beckett appeared.[17] This also deals with *Watt*, although not in detail. His observation that "of all strenuous lives, the contemplative life is the most strenuous" is worthy of note (p. 512). All Beckett's protagonists, including Watt and Sam, are said to be similar. In Morse's opinion, we have here a type of unity in character which is

16. "Beckett by the Madeleine," *Columbia Forum* 4 (1961):21–25.
17. "The Contemplative Life According to Samuel Beckett," *Hudson Review* 15 (1962/63):512–24.

not formal, but rather metaphysical. In terms of content, we have not a relationship of various plots, but rather "recurrent symbols" (p. 514). Morse writes:

> For notwithstanding the whimsical and ambiguous disclaimer at the end of *Watt*, "No symbols where none intended", Beckett's novels are forests of symbols, artfully planted, tended and intended . . . (p. 515)

> The protagonists all walk or crawl with difficulty, being pilgrims in this world; they all play games of permutation, vainly seeking that perfect distribution in which alone True Justice consists; they all prefer the contemplative to the active life; they are all scorned by the active world, and altogether they have so many habits, attitudes and afflictions in common that I suspect that we have to do with a series of metempsychoses or eternal returns. (P. 515)

Like all Beckett's protagonists, Watt suffers from the disease "of seeing everything whole, under the aspect of eternity . . ."—a disease "that unfits us for mortality" (p. 522).

Two thematic studies of *Watt* appeared in 1963 and 1964. The first, by Sidney Warhaft, is entitled "Threne and Theme in *Watt*."[18] The second, by Susan Field Senneff, also specializes in matters of content.[19] Senneff studies the various songs in *Watt*, beginning with the one Watt hears after he has rolled into the ditch. The author is convinced that the music continues what can no longer be expressed in words: "The form of the music not only parallels the events of Watt's life, but carries the themes to their conclusion" (p. 149). Neither article, however, is directly related to the theme of my study, because

18. *Wisconsin Studies in Contemporary Literature* 4 (1963):261–78.
19. "Song and Music in Samuel Beckett's *Watt*," *Modern Fiction Studies* 10 (1964):137–49.

each views the content of *Watt* from a very narrow angle. Senneff concludes: "Even if the Threne music is unrelated to the text, it means something: it means boredom and unrelation . . . The rest is silence" (p. 149).

Closer to the theme of the present gnosiological study is Alvin Greenberg's article in *Criticism* which deals with the death of the soul.[20] Greenberg remarks at the outset that insurmountable difficulties are encountered when one wishes to understand the character of the protagonist Watt. Watt behaves more "as a thing in motion" than as "a sentient being" (p. 1). He enters Mr. Knott's house without any preparation whatever and is himself a being with little if any reality. The question "What is Watt?" is unanswerable to begin with; how much more so, then, is the question of what he experiences. The only certainty is that the process of dying is a route to the inner self, a common theme of contemporary literature. Greenberg indulges in a bit of psychological phenomenology and refers to J. J. Buytendijk when he writes, "Human reality is equivalent to being conscious, and this can be defined only as open to the world, as cast upon the world" (p. 4). In the psyche, Greenberg concludes, the human being can be defined only hypothetically. Phenomenological analysis can be carried out only on the basis of examples. With regard to *Watt*, this means "we may see that the dwindling Watt, into the depths of whose psyche we are permitted few intimate glimpses, is eminently susceptible to analysis through the phenomenological approach: that Watt's own problem, in fact, is given a phenomenological structure" (p. 9).

Greenberg interprets *Watt* as a book that conveys experience but makes no effort to harmonize this experience with reason (p. 14). This can be seen as a starting point for understanding the independent reality of Mr. Knott's peculiar world versus other realms of experience, but Greenberg does not attempt this in his article. Yet the author does refer to pure

---

20. "The Death of the Psyche: A Way to the Self in the Contemporary Novel," *Criticism* 8 (1966):1–18.

existence, the pure being of later protagonists such as those that appear in the trilogy.

Ann M. Trivisonno (1969)[21] sees in the very names "Watt" and "Knott" references to the epistemological meaning of the novel: "Watt in search of the *whatness* of things encounters Knott or *nothingness*" (p. 29). In her opinion, Beckett presents in this work his vision of the existential dilemma of modern man, specifically by means of Watt's metaphorical journey to Mr. Knott's estate. Especially in the third part of *Watt*, she sees an attack by Beckett on language and reason. "By assigning the narrative responsibility to the lunatic Sam, Beckett can relate the quest in an order which is deliberately distorting and confusing" (p. 35). She sees Watt's journey as a solipsistic affair, which simply means that there is no universal meaning in it. Beckett is just going around in circles, and it exhausts the artistic meaning of the whole to say that the journey represents Beckett's paradoxical theory of creativity "through the metaphor of the quest."

Ludovic Janvier (1969),[22] the translator of *Watt* into French, sees *Watt* as a *Bildungsroman* (p. 312). In his interpretation, Watt undergoes a breakthrough experience. According to Janvier, Watt is Beckett's first surviving protagonist, since Murphy dies at the end of the novel of that name. At the end of his difficult time at Mr. Knott's house, Watt stands there, "figure tournée vers l'absence et l'oubli, mais rejetée dans la présence et l'éveil douloureux" (p. 323).

Because of the number of relationships which can be established between the article by John J. Mood (1971)[23] and my interpretation of *Watt*, I mention the article only briefly here. I will discuss Mood's ideas in detail in chapter 3 in order to clarify my own position. Mood sees in *Watt* a criticism of existentialism and positivism through the attempt to create an

21. "Meaning and Function of the Quest in Beckett's *Watt*," *Critique* 12 (Minneapolis, 1969):28–38.

22. "Les difficultés d'un séjour," *Critique* 263 (Paris, 1969):312–23.

23. " 'The Personal System'—Samuel Beckett's *Watt*," *PMLA* 86 (1971):255–65.

original system, even though this system is doomed to failure. "*Watt* has portrayed the equal failure of rationality to provide an internal system of any validity or use" (p. 264).

François Martel (1972)[24] studies the game-playing aspect of the novel through mathematical analysis of the so-called series. This represents a major contribution to our understanding of the formal side of *Watt*, but it fails to coax anything from the content of the novel which might illuminate the gnosiological aspect that lies beyond these fascinating games of logic.

Eleanor Swanson (1971/72)[25] sees primarily the broken time structure in *Watt*. She believes that Beckett, by means of the new arrangement of chapters given at the beginning of part IV of *Watt*, is attempting to lead the reader forward and backward in time: "The time-sequence of the narrative has been reordered, and the reader, like Watt, has been walking backwards and forward through time. Past, present, and future are confused and the logical relationships between them are negated" (p. 268). This is in fact an essential insight.

John Chalker (1975)[26] considers *Watt* a complex satire and believes that it is an "exercise in absurdity" (p. 21). A comparison with Sterne and Swift illustrates his position that Beckett has written an unconventional novel, the essence of which is to be understood as satire. Unlike other critics, Chalker sees Watt as a very human figure. I will return to Chalker's essay in chapter 4.

Jerry Wassermann (1977)[27] defends the viewpoint that Watt constructs his own world of words, where he finds consolation in semantics. The brilliant formal aspects which char-

---

24. "Jeux formels dans *Watt*," *Poétique* 10 (1972):153–75.

25. "Samuel Beckett's *Watt*: A Coming and A Going," *Modern Fiction Studies* 17 (1971):264–68.

26. "The Satiric Shape of *Watt*," in *Beckett the Shape Changer*, ed. Katherine Worth (London, 1975), pp. 21–37.

27. "Watt's World of Words," in *Twentieth-Century Poetry, Fiction, Theory*, ed. Harry R. Garvin (Lewisburgh, Pa., and London, 1977), pp. 123–38.

acterize this complex work are put in relief in this study, but it provides no further commentary.

Mathew Winston (1977)[28] uses the first footnote in *Watt* to analyze the unique character of the book. After the first pages of *Watt*, which emanate from a still traditional, omniscient narrator, the narrative point of view changes radically, a change to which the first footnote refers. Winston sees in *Watt* "a fiction which does not imitate the reader's world and therefore is not bound by its rules" (p. 81). I will return again in chapter 4 to Winston's opinion that *Watt* is primarily a comic work whose character is playful rather than "didactic."

In the *Journal of Beckett Studies* (1979),[29] Thomas J. Cousineau discusses Beckett's language in *Watt*. For him as well, the novel represents primarily an abstract work of language that makes no direct statement. The language in *Watt* has the function of forbidding and consoling; it is largely its own end, not a means to an end. Many critics approach Beckett's oeuvre in this way.

We have thus completed a preliminary survey of all articles whose primary subject is *Watt*. The section below discusses publications devoted to Beckett's prose works as a whole which therefore also include comments on *Watt*.

CRITICAL STUDIES OF BECKETT

The earliest and most comprehensive work of this type is John Fletcher's *The Novels of Samuel Beckett* (1964).[30] For Fletcher, *Watt* is primarily "a strange and enigmatic story," less precise than *Murphy* (p. 62). As for Mr. Knott's house, Fletcher remarks that it is as if it were located "nowhere." As a character, Watt is clearly associated with his predecessors, as is the case with all Beckett's subsequent protagonists.

28. "*Watt*'s First Footnote," *Journal of Modern Literature* 6 (1977):69–82.

29. "*Watt*: Language as Interdiction and Consolation," *Journal of Beckett Studies*, no. 4 (1979), pp. 1–13.

30. 2d ed. (London, 1970), pp. 59–89.

Fletcher sees Watt as "a reincarnation of Murphy" (p. 63). In spite of this, Watt remains a "rather shadowy figure"; "apart from his confused tale to Sam, he speaks only three or four times in the book" (p. 63). "He moreover prefers, like Murphy, to 'see in his own dark', and is a 'sullen silent sot . . . always musing', either talking to himself, or listening to voices which whisper and sing to him continually" (p. 65).

Fletcher notes with insight that "Murphy's retreat is spoken of in semi-visual terms . . . and Watt's in terms of hearing, of listening to an inner discourse" (p. 66), but in much of what *Watt* offers the reader, Fletcher sees only mystification. He considers the formal peculiarities of the book in this way also. "Most events in the book are narrated at fussy, unnecessary length," he believes, and yet he confirms Beckett's "fastidious completeness and extreme precision," which immediately impress any reader of *Watt* (p. 72). Fletcher adds, "This exhaustiveness frequently has a nightmarish quality about it." These stylistic peculiarities constitute the humor of the book. The digressions are reminiscent of Sterne's *Tristram Shandy*. Other aspects, such as the gaps in the manuscript, also recall Swift's *Tale of a Tub*. Fletcher discusses the philosophical content of *Watt* as well, but he is convinced that Watt achieves the emptiness of rejection from the world only after his period of residence in Mr. Knott's house. Mr. Knott's house and garden have destroyed for him the world of things, logic, and the meaning of names (p. 78). On the other hand, Fletcher believes that "Watt has come to Mr. Knott's house fundamentally for religious reasons" (p. 81), "but the results, on the whole, were meagre" (p. 84) because Watt's knowledge of Mr. Knott at the end is zero. Watt remains "the eternal question what?" (p. 86). In an addendum to the Watt chapter, Fletcher corrects Jacqueline Hoefer's assumption that the ladder story refers to Wittgensteins's *Tractatus Logico-Philosophicus*. Samuel Beckett told Fletcher that the image of the ladder is derived from "a Welsh joke" and asserted in 1961 that he had read Wittgenstein's works only in the preceding two years (pp. 87–88). Commenting on Ruby Cohn's essay on

Watt and Kafka's *The Castle*, Fletcher states that Beckett had indeed read Kafka's books at that time in German, but that *Watt* was a much more comical work than *The Castle*. There are great stylistic differences between these works as well. Ruby Cohn had also drawn attention to Kafka's classic narrative form; Beckett himself commented that "it goes on like a steam-roller" (p. 89). Fletcher assumes, however, that both *Watt* and *The Castle* represent myths, which means "it is we who lend the symbol meaning, from our own hopes and fears" (p. 89).

Raymond Federman (1965)[31] discusses Beckett's early novels from the aspect of a journey into chaos. In many ways he is close to John Fletcher's critical standpoint. The two authors have brought out a joint publication, *Samuel Beckett: His Works and His Critics* (1970).[32]

An early article by Melvin J. Friedman (1960)[33] deals with Beckett's novels, including *Watt*. He views the element of the new in relation to Joyce and Proust. This is valid if one is trying to fit Beckett into the development of the psychological novel, but it certainly fails to penetrate to the heart of the matter. Friedman is guilty of a few errors. He states, for example, that Beckett was about to marry Joyce's daughter and that he was Joyce's "secretary." In regard to *Watt*, he believes "it indicates no 'new direction' in the novel form" (p. 52); he sees in the work only that "*Watt* carries the plotless novel to new lengths; unfortunately, it seems to be a stopping place" (p. 52). If we think of the subsequent novels that Beckett wrote in French, especially the trilogy, this opinion certainly cannot be defended.

Olga Bernal (1976)[34] proceeds from Beckett's own words

31. *Journey to Chaos: Samuel Beckett's Early Fiction* (Berkeley and Los Angeles, 1965).

32. Berkeley and Los Angeles, 1970.

33. "The Novels of Samuel Beckett: An Amalgam of Joyce and Proust," *Comparative Literature* 12 (1960):47–58.

34. "Das Dilemma der Repräsentation," in *Materialien zu Samuel Becketts Romanen*, ed. Engelhardt and Mettler.

on the work of his painter friend Bram van Velde. What Beckett says about "representation" applies not just to painting but to his literary work as well. The expression of the inexpressible—that is the challenge Beckett faces. His characters cannot in fact be represented by traditional vocabulary. These words have no power over them. Beckett's characters thus exist in the "shadow of the words" (p. 202).

Ursula Dreysse (1970)[35] has published a comprehensive study of the structural principles and content of Beckett's novels which includes a discussion of *Watt* (pp. 28ff). In *Watt* she still finds traces of traditional patterns, but she basically sees a progressive transformation of the traditional form of the novel. Linear narrative structure is abandoned. In her opinion, the sequence of the four parts should correspond to the order 1, 2, 4, 3—an order not suggested by Beckett anywhere in the novel. Her reasoning is as follows: "The fourth chapter again introduces Watt and chronologically comes before the third, because in the third chapter Watt is already in the asylum, whereas in the fourth chapter the asylum is called the goal of his journey" (p. 29). The present study of the gnosiological aspect of *Watt* does not follow this interpretation, as will be shown in chapters 3 and 4. Dreysse sees Watt as a human figure in the process of disintegration. "Watt is no longer physically intact; he is physically grotesque, a predecessor of the crippled and immobile heroes of the French trilogy" (p.30). The category of action is replaced by that of situation (p. 31). Watt's naïve nominalism is doomed to failure. Dreysse sees in Watt "the first signs of a consciousness of the opacity and unintelligibility of our world, which becomes ever stronger in the course of Beckett's works" (p. 32). "At the end of this process is Watt's speech mannerism of inversion, which destroys both language and meaning"

35. *Realtät als Aufgabe. Eine Untersuchung über Aufbaugesetze und Gehalt des Romanwerks von Samuel Beckett* (Bad Homburg v.d.H., Berlin, Zürich, 1970).

(p. 33). The author takes all of this as signs of general skepticism and a clear awareness of crisis. The nightmarish quality of existence does not lead, however, to an abandonment of the search for meaning or for a more intelligible reality (p. 34).

Eugene Webb, in his book on Beckett's novels (1970),[36] supports the opinion also shared by Cohn and others that much of the atmosphere in *Watt* is reminiscent of Kafka's *The Castle*. He then discusses in detail the reasons that motivated Beckett to write his later novels in French. Webb sees *Watt* as primarily a parody of Dante's *Paradiso* in *The Divine Comedy*. He is still convinced, however, that Watt does not seek death but simply becomes insane (p. 25). His comparison of Geulincx and Descartes with the dualistic world view described in *Watt* is worthy of attention (pp. 26ff.) but does not compensate for his belief in Watt's insanity. In later sections of his book, Webb makes it clear that he considers Mr. Knott a parody of God: all the numberless souls who, like Watt, come to Mr. Knott's house leave it with the same disillusionment (pp. 60–61). Webb's general opinion is that the novel is a transitional work. After Watt has researched "the traditional fields of human knowledge" and has become disillusioned, he is transformed, so to speak, into Beckett's next protagonist (p. 69).

Klaus Birkenhauer (1971),[37] who sees Beckett's heroes as outsiders, discusses *Watt* on pp. 70ff. of his monograph. He points out that Beckett began to speak his *own* language in *Watt*, even before he switched to writing in French. Birkenhauer then reviews the content of *Watt*, devoting a good deal of attention to the musical passages. By suggesting that the plot could ultimately be taking place in an internment camp, he provides an alternative to the one-sided interpretation of the action as occurring in an insane asylum. This hardly threatens the status of the hospital idea, and Birkenhauer himself admits that his interpretation does not lead anywhere: "If Watt . . . is insane, or becomes insane in the course of his

---

36. *Samuel Beckett: A Study of His Novels* (London, 1970).
37. *Beckett* (Reinbek bei Hamburg, 1971).

narrative, the entire novel would then be nothing more than a three-hundred-page crazy joke exaggerated in all respects by an amanuensis just as insane as Watt" (p. 77). He regards part III as a distorted reflection of part II. Overall, Birkenhauer believes that *Watt* is an "exploratory exercise in language" (p. 79).

Horst Breuer (1972)[38] finds parallels between the linguistic peculiarities in *Watt* and the speech mannerisms of schizophrenics and sees this bizarre element taken to its extreme in part III of the novel (pp. 157–58). On the basis of citations from *Murphy, How It Is,* and *Watt,* he shows that Beckett has an above-average understanding of psychology. "Even if the parallelism between literary work and experimental psychology were completely and entirely unconscious, Beckett would still remain the spokesman for an age whose spirit has been formed, among other things, by modern science and the anthropological disciplines . . . But it is doubtless a biographical question rather than a problem of literary criticism to decide how conscious or unconscious the process of artistic creation was in Beckett's case" (p. 43). I will return to another point in Breuer's book in my discussion of Watt's experiences in the waiting room of the train station.

Alfred Alvarez (1973)[39] considers *Watt* a definite dead end. He attests to the work's abstractness and mild insanity (p. 44). It is a work of "midlife crisis." He therefore adopts what must be termed an extreme point of view, even among the opinions of critics who consider *Watt* a story from a madhouse.

Rolf Breuer (1976)[40] discusses *Watt* in two long passages in which he points out the difficulties that confront the unprepared reader (pp. 9–24, 62–80). Beckett, in fact, takes no account of "informational redundancy and the limits of 'good

38. *Samuel Beckett* (Munich, 1972).
39. *Beckett* (London, 1978).
40. *Die Kunst der Paradoxie* (Munich, 1976).

taste' " (pp. 63–64). I will return to a few comments in this book in chapter 3.

James Knowlson and John Pilling, the editors of the *Journal of Beckett Studies*, do not discuss *Watt* directly in their book, *Frescoes of the Skull* (1979),[41] because they deal only with the late prose and plays. Their book is of such great importance for an understanding of Beckett's prose as a whole, however, that it should be mentioned here. The title of the book, as the authors write in the foreword, is "an adequate description of any one of Beckett's works" (p. xiii). They report that Beckett himself characterized his way of writing as "onto-speleology."

A book published in 1980 by Eric P. Levy entitled *Beckett and the Voice of Species*[42] contains a chapter on *Watt* which deals with its narrative structure and the problem of subjectivity. Levy first discusses two intellectual movements from which interpreters of *Watt* have hoped to find help: Wittgenstein's positivism and the structuralism of linguists. He is convinced, however, that both directions can contribute to only a limited extent to an explanation of this novel, whereas the central question of the identity of Watt remains unanswered. The original narrator "drops out," and Watt loses his foothold in the external world. Watt is, in fact, forced to rely on the testimony of others in order to exist. Without witnesses he enters an experiential realm of nothingness. "This is precisely the case as soon as Watt crosses the threshold of Mr. Knott's house" (p. 30). Levy concludes that Watt is no ordinary person: "Watt is reduced to a finite centre around which the experience flows. He is not so much a self as merely the place where experience is registered" (p. 31). Levy is entirely correct in seeing in *Watt* "a perfect homogeneous flux" (p. 35); he thus rebukes those critics who complain that the structure of *Watt* is too loose. He is of the opinion that "the novel

41. *Frescoes of the Skull: The Later Prose and Drama of Samuel Beckett* (London, 1979).

42. *Beckett and the Voice of Species: A Study of the Prose Fiction* (Totowa, N.J., and Dublin, 1980), pp. 27–38.

presents Watt not as an independent character but rather as a mirror image of the narrator behind him" (p. 36). Levy's view of Beckett's evolution as a narrator is also important: "With each new novel, Beckettian narration expresses more seriously the absence of subjectivity that the experience of Nothing entails" (p. 36).

Looking back over the secondary literature on *Watt*, we can conclude that the authors employ formal criteria almost exclusively and that they come to the unanimous conclusion that *Watt* takes place in a mental hospital. In many cases they consider both Watt and Sam to be insane. In the form in which it is usually presented, this mental hospital theory is unacceptable. Shifting the scene to an internment camp, as Klaus Birkenhauer recommends, is not a convincing solution. The various discussions of narrative point of view, however, are of great interest. All the authors emphasize the absurd character and breakup of the narrative structure. Linear time is abandoned at the beginning of part I, and in part III it is transformed into its complete opposite. The view of Eleanor Swanson that as human beings we, like Watt, are forced to accept the universe as "incongruous and unknowable" in order to survive also appears to me to be off target.

Past approaches to *Watt* have either failed to ask what existential content the novel may have to offer or have failed to take this question seriously enough. As soon as *Watt*'s conventional tie to reality is broken—as indicated by the interruption or reversal of the natural chronology—most authors content themselves with the observation that this must now be the story of a madman or a description of his world of experience. As a starting point for an explanation of Watt, various philosophers are cited, such as early Wittgenstein on logic. Others compare the fundamental problems in Beckett with the thought of Descartes or his follower Geulincx, Heidegger, or even Aristotle. One has the impression, however, that even the classical philosophers are unable to help.

Rolf Breuer avoids this problem with an elegant twist. In his opinion, Beckett is less interested in presenting reality in *Watt* than he is in exploring the possibilities of knowing and interpreting reality: "There is no doubt that Beckett fails in his attempt to present the failure of a quest for a transcendence which does not exist. But because this failure is predetermined by the definition of the problem, then the real issue from the very beginning is therefore to fail, so to speak, as intelligently as possible."[43] In view of the precarious epistemological situation, the only choice for the author is to behave as a schizophrenic, and "the only adequate artistic principle . . . is (highly abstract) irony."[44]

The present study rejects not only the mental hospital theory, but also the opinion that much can be gained from comparisons of this complex work and individual philosophical systems. It is impossible that it was ever Beckett's intention to provide a literary commentary on any philosophical system. Comparisons of this type fail even to approach the existential character of the work, and no philosophy is able to "explain" it. In view of my attempt to uncover the gnosiological basis of Beckett's *Watt*, it seems appropriate to point out this difficult situation now. My opinion has evolved precisely from a study of the secondary literature. Epistemological and especially hermeneutic aspects of *Watt* have been neglected in most cases as a result of this difficulty. The only exception here is a brief survey of the content and meaning of *Watt* published by Marie Renate Büttner in 1978.[45] She considers Beckett's novel from the same anthropological standpoint as my study and accordingly, although without detailed justification, comes to similar conclusions.

---

43. *Die Kunst der Paradoxie,* pp. 79–80.
44. Ibid.
45. *"Watt* von Samuel Beckett," *Die Christengemeinschaft* 50 (1978): 63–65.

The Translations of Watt *into French and German*

I will discuss problems that have to do with the translation of
the original English *Watt* only to the extent that they are related to questions bearing on the central theme of my study.
In my heuristic research I was able to make use of two translations which were made with Beckett's assistance. The 1969
French edition was translated by Ludovic and Agnes Janvier
with Beckett's extensive help. Although not all the critics were
satisfied with this translation, as Deirdre Bair reports,[46] the
author himself was. The somewhat later German translation
was prepared by Elmar Tophoven in very close collaboration
with Beckett. As he explained in a paper presented before the
Akademie der Künste in Berlin in October 1973, Tophoven
was able to rely on the English and French editions as on
"two originals."[47] Through this close collaboration with Beckett, who has a good command of German, a third authentic
text came into being. In the paper just mentioned, "En traduisant Beckett," Tophoven points out that any translation is
obviously a primary interpretation, even though, in contrast
to more comprehensive attempts at interpretation, it has
narrow formal limits. An example of the difficulties continually encountered in the translation of *Watt* is provided by
Tophoven in his discussion.[48]

When Beckett himself translates his works into one or
the other of the languages in which he is accustomed to write,
he keeps very close to the original, that is, for example, either
to the English text, as in *Watt*, or to the French, as in the case
of the trilogy. This is associated with the fact that in the creative act of writing, form and content are experienced as a

46. *Samuel Beckett: A Biography*, p. 594.

47. This paper is found under the title, "En traduisant Beckett," in *Das
Werk Samuel Becketts: Berliner Colloquium*, ed. Hans Mayer and Uwe Johnson
(Frankfurt am Main, 1975), pp. 159ff. Tophoven has thus provided an insight
into Samuel Beckett's "school for translators" and expressed his "thanks to
the most patient of his teachers" (p. 173).

48. Ibid., p. 167.

unity.[49] Deviations from the original are thus attributable not to the translator but to the languages themselves, that is, to their idiomatic expressions, their specific associations implied by certain expressions and their connotative differences, and the sound value and rhythm of the words. Compromises and certain inadequacies are unavoidable. In many cases, such differences in the translations can also be helpful in interpreting the original. They are indications of something which is in itself "unsayable" but which could somehow be concealed in Beckett's works.

This is an appropriate place to refer to Beckett's sobering remark, "Every word is a lie."[50] There is more in this statement than just the general observation that literature, as a product of the imagination, is a "lie." There is something of Beckett's conscientiousness in it, his often-cited "meticulousness." The striving for precision and the purity of the word or expression is characteristic of Beckett. If someone whose means of expression is the word says that "every word is a lie," this must mean that a (concrete) experience precedes the word, and that the forming of the word, that is, the translation into language, must already represent a loss in relation

49. Asked about the duality of form and content, Beckett said that in the creative act there is only a unity and that no separation is possible (April 12, 1969). (All my conversations with Beckett are documented in extensive notes, which have been checked and supplemented as necessary by other participants.)

50. Beckett made this remark (originally, "Jedes Wort ist eine Lüge") at the end of a conversation about the so-called "nothingness." It was difficult, he said, to express the content of this experience. It occurs at a very deep level within himself. Words are of no use in expressing what happens there, where it is calm, still, and simple. It is a real problem that it is impossible to convey these relationships accurately. One should actually remain silent, but at the same time there is the compulsion to speak. That is the terrible thing—to be unable and yet to be compelled. This discordance is a real dilemma. I remarked that he had succeeded in expressing the truth by discovering a way to use words, arranging them one after the other, even though the individual words themselves might not be exact. Beckett answered, "That's the dream!" (Berlin, September 10, 1967; original conversation in German).

to the "inexpressible" spiritual reality out of which the word is created. Necessarily, the act of formulation is often agonizing. "If it wasn't for the compulsion to speak, I would rather be silent," he once confessed.[51]

For Beckett, as for many other writers, writing is not a pleasure; it is a duty to be fulfilled with the greatest dedication.[52] For him there was never any question of whether he should write or not; he continued to work even when he failed to find a publisher for his trilogy. "When my teaching career went sour," he once confessed, looking back, "there were only two choices for me: to write or to do nothing."[53]

Beckett has never had any patience with platitudes, and his love of detail and careful working methods are known. One of Clov's comic responses seems typical of the author's attitude: Clov is about to tell Hamm what is going on in the outside world, but before he looks through the telescope he

51. Conversation in Ussy on April 12, 1969. Ionesco's attitude also suggests that "every word is a lie." He writes in his diary: "Words no longer demonstrate: they chatter. Words are literary. They are an escape. They stop silence from speaking. They deafen you . . . Silence is golden. It ought to serve as a guarantee for speech. Alas, we've got inflation" (*Fragments of a Journal*, trans. Jean Stewart [New York, 1968], p. 73).

Eugène Ionesco, who has frequently expressed his esteem for Beckett (e.g., in conversations with Claude Bonnefoy), is also highly appreciated by Beckett. Although according to Beckett he (Beckett) has met Ionesco only "by accident," he likes his plays, especially *The Chairs* and passages from *Exit the King* (Paris, May 27, 1967). He also praised Ionesco's story, "Le véritable bordel," which he had read (February 22, 1975).

52. Charles Monteith, Director of the London publishing house of Faber and Faber (and therefore a successor to T. S. Eliot), describes Beckett as "courteous, punctilious, unfailingly prompt, most scrupulous, most sensitive in his concern with meticulous textual accuracy." (See *Beckett at 60: A Festschrift* [London, 1967], p. 87.)

53. April 12, 1969 in Ussy. A typical Beckettian understatement, for his teaching career at Trinity College in Dublin and at the Ecole Normale Superieure in Paris was completely successful, as eyewitnesses have reported, even though his teaching methods were highly unorthodox. Beckett had a very promising career as an academic teacher to look forward to, but at the beginning of the 1930s he abandoned it of his own volition. (See Bair, *Samuel Beckett: A Biography*, p. 123.)

asks, "Any particular sections you fancy? Or merely the whole thing?"[54] The "whole thing" is simply not enough.

Beckett's obsession with detail in *Watt* can occasionally get on the reader's nerves, but a good part of its humor is based on unnecessarily painstaking description:

> If Watt's mouth was open, and his jaw sunk, and his eyes glassy, and his head sunk, and his knees bent, and his back bent, his mind was busy, busy wondering which was best, to shut the door, from which he felt the draught, on the nape, of his neck, and set down his bags, and sit down, or to shut the door, and set down his bags, without sitting down, or to shut the door, and sit down, without setting down his bags.[55]

As difficult as it is to translate his works, Beckett's indefatigable care and love of detail are ultimately of benefit to the work of translation. It is not only his own translations which are models of the art. He has, through the aspects of his personality mentioned above, also helped others dedicated to the translation of his works to achieve the greatest possible accuracy. Just as Tophoven was able to rely on the English and French editions of *Watt* in developing his own "primary interpretation," that is, the German edition, the study presented here has been able to derive support from all three texts either written by Beckett or authorized by him.

Esoteric Quality, Form as "Bodying Forth," and Gnosiological Content

Beckett's deceased friend A. J. Leventhal spoke of an "esoteric quality" in Beckett's work.[56] Many readers or spectators re-

54. Samuel Beckett, *Endgame: A Play in One Act* (New York, 1958); reprinted in *The Collected Works of Samuel Beckett* (New York, 1970), p. 73.

55. Samuel Beckett, *Watt* (New York: Grove Press, 1959), pp. 220–21. All further page references to *Watt* are from this edition.

56. "There is a certain esoteric quality hidden skeletally in Beckett's work." See n. 1.

spond to this quality, even if the phrase is associated with many different meanings. It is not easy to define what is really meant by it, for it is the very nature of the esoteric to be obscure—it would be a contradiction if this quality could be defined precisely. The word esoteric means secret, hidden, or encoded, but it also refers in Greek philosophy to that which can be understood only after appropriate mental training— that is, initiation. The word will be used here exclusively in this latter sense. If we also take Leventhal's term "skeletally" or "hidden skeletally," which is equally pertinent, we can come close to the meaning of the statement which I have chosen as the epigraph for this introductory chapter: as though by a skeleton, Beckett's work is supported internally by this esoteric quality.

Because this "inner substance" is hidden, it is easy to overlook. It is possible to negate evidence of it simply by calling efforts to produce such evidence mere speculation. And if we remember that Beckett has often been called a nihilist, it is easy to understand that others can also consider him "aspiritual," that is, a rationalist. Both opinions are incorrect.[57] It is true that Beckett's work appeals to the intellect, but

57. Characteristic of the nihilist is not just the denial of universal values and knowledge (or of social orders). Out of conviction, a nihilist has come to terms with his ignorance and has therefore given up even dealing with the problems of knowledge and truth. In this regard, DuBois-Reymond's description of traditional nineteenth-century science applies equally to the nihilist's attitude: "ignoramus, ignorabimus." Beckett never made an "act of faith" of this sort. Even though he appears in conversation to lack interest in some of those questions, he obviously considers that deeper experience and knowledge are possible. In totally dead-end, hopeless situations, his characters show an enormous amount of toughness and stoic persistence. In a conversation in Berlin on September 9, 1967, when I asked him if he believed in "positive nothingness," he answered "Yes, of course." He even stood up and paced back and forth in the room, saying, "I simply cannot understand why some people call me a nihilist. There is no basis for that. After all, Hamm says (Beckett quoted the phrase in German), 'where it is green beyond the hills'—and after a short pause, 'if there is anything green.' " (Literally this passage in *Endgame* reads: "But beyond the hills? Eh?

because it continually transcends the rational plane, as abstract painting does, it is also spiritual. There is no doubt that his characterization of Proust's artistic tendency applies equally to his own: "the only possible spiritual development is in the sense of depth."[58]

If many spectators or readers respond to Beckett's works as being essentially negative, this is to some extent the result of their own passivity, or they confuse pessimism with nihilism. Beckett is no optimist—he sees things as they are. And it is not his intention to entertain or teach. He once described himself, "Je ne suis pas un intellectuel. Je ne suis que sensibilité."[59]

In the depths of the soul, words no longer exist. The dilemma consists in trying to use words to express what is experienced there. As reported by Martin Esslin, Niklaus Gessner is said to have asked Beckett whether his writing did not contradict his obvious conviction that language is incapable of conveying meaning. Gessner received the reply, "Que voulez-vous, Monsieur? C'est les mots; on n'a rien d'autre." Esslin concludes, "Beckett's entire work can be seen as a

Perhaps it's still green. Eh? . . . Perhaps you won't need to go very far" [p. 39].)

On another occasion, Beckett said that he sees his role as one of "provoking questions." He cannot supply answers. Artistic creation is a question of "sensitivity," or of the "finding of forms." This agrees with what Alan Schneider has quoted Beckett as saying: "I take no sides. I am interested in the shape of ideas." (See *Beckett at 60*, p. 34.) I was somewhat surprised to hear Siegfried Melchinger express his opinion in a short conversation at the Hofgeismar Protestant Academy that Beckett was a "rationalist." No one doubts that he is also a rationalist, but that he is only a rationalist must be emphatically denied.

58. Samuel Beckett, *Proust* (London, 1931; New York, [1957]), pp. 46ff. In the original text, the complete passage reads as follows: "For the artist, who does not deal in surfaces, the rejection of friendship is not only reasonable, but a necessity. Because the only possible spiritual development is in the sense of depth. The artistic tendency is not expansive, but a contraction. And art is the apotheosis of solitude."

59. Reported by Gabriele d'Aubarède in "En attendant . . . Beckett," *Nouvelles littéraires*, February 16, 1961, p. 7.

search for the reality that lies behind mere reasoning in conceptual terms."[60] In the deepest layers of the mind, where creative work is done, it can hardly be said that total clarity reigns. There is, rather, only a mysterious darkness,[61] in which all has become calm, simple, and "nameless."[62]

The discovery of form is a component of this bodying forth out of airy nothing.[63] The question is, the bodying forth of what? (of *Watt?*) Even if Beckett once believed in his earlier years in "pure" art, as when he spoke about his friend the painter Bram van Velde and his nonreferential art,[64] in Beckett's case we are still dealing with an art which is not neutral in terms of values. His assertion that abstract painting is "pure" is not convincing, because it has been understood for some time that this art movement was quite capable of making a statement. Reduction in this context does not mean loss—it

60. *The Theatre of the Absurd,* 2d rev. ed. (Garden City, N.Y., 1969), p. 64.

61. In *Murphy* Beckett describes three zones of consciousness, which he identifies by the words "light," "semidark," and "dark," but which he does not associate with ethical values. I discuss these three zones of consciousness in chapter 4 of this study. The zone termed "dark" here is the one in which Murphy's spirit can move about freely like a "mote" and which he describes as a "matrix of surds." See *Murphy* (New York, 1957), p. 11.

62. In reference to the last volume of his trilogy (*The Unnamable*), Beckett answered my direct question as to why he did not give the main character a name in the following way: "It is simply because no name turned up for him during the writing. There's no explanation. His identity was lost in the confrontation with nothingness" (Berlin, September 9, 1967; see also n. 50).

63. In *A Midsummer Night's Dream* (act 5, sc. 1, lines 12–17), Shakespeare has Theseus say the following to describe the creative act of the poet:

> The poet's eye, in a fine frenzy rolling,
> Doth glance from heaven to earth, from earth to heaven;
> And as imagination bodies forth
> The forms of things unknown, the poet's pen
> Turns them to shapes, and gives to airy nothing
> A local habitation and a name.

64. Samuel Beckett and George Duthuit, *Bram van Velde* (London, 1965). See also Engelhardt and Mettler, *Materialien zu Samuel Becketts Romanen,* pp. 18ff.

can also be a form of intensification if it focuses our attention on the essential.

Today the debate on the moral neutrality of art is generally considered to have run its course. Every word that is written down changes the world, whether the author wishes it or not. It has already been made clear from the preceding discussion that in Beckett's works we are not dealing with "information" pertaining to external (e.g., historical) or peripheral mental events and even less with an art relevant to the present in the sense of propaganda for a specific world view. Bertolt Brecht's failure in his attempt to reinterpret *Waiting for Godot* as a work of social criticism is well known.

Beckett writes from the deepest level of his inner life; at the same time, however, his writing cannot be called subjective. Otherwise, he would be unable to reach levels in the reader or spectator which have such universal existential meaning. He achieves this impression of objectivity through the rigor of his forms, realism, and total honesty with himself. He is a purist with regard to this "realism." Over the course of his life he has distanced himself ever more strictly from his own external world of experience to acquire the freedom to concentrate more effectively on the essential. He has not made it easier on himself or on others. To an ever greater extent, writing has become for him a conscious placing of words. Tophoven confirms this on the basis of his translation work, which became more difficult and more time-consuming the shorter Beckett's texts became.[65] A symbol of Beckett's striving for purity and selflessness of expression is his adoption of the French language. The American director Herbert Blau once accused Beckett of writing in a foreign language in order to hide certain aspects of his character. Beckett confirmed this: yes, there were some things in him which he didn't like; French had the right "weakening" effect.[66] Since the trilogy, Beckett has written in his native language only

65. See "En traduisant Beckett," p. 159.
66. Esslin, *Theatre of the Absurd*, p. 19.

rarely and, so to speak, only for recreation. Esslin remarks, "Works like Beckett's, which spring from the deepest strata of the mind, . . . would be destroyed by the slightest suggestion of glibness or facility; they must be the outcome of a painful struggle with the medium of their expression."[67]

Total lack of sentimentality and brevity of form are evidence of the rigorous principles to which Beckett submits himself. Nothing superfluous is tolerated. Everything is subordinated to the first principle, purity of form. This purity is an expression of his truthfulness. It is reflected in Beckett's way of life, which is focused on the essential, and in his personal modesty, punctuality, and fairness.[68]

The "weakening effect," a form of "veiling" of the personal (even if it slips in only by way of the peculiarities which are inherent in the native language of every human being), has nothing to do with what we have called the "esoteric quality." On the contrary, it appears that this quality manifests itself fully only after the "all-too-personal" has been left out. Through the connection between the various fictitious names (Murphy, Watt, Molloy, Malone, etc.) and Beckett's signature ("Sam"), Leventhal discovered a mysterious concordance between the person and the object of the description, but this is only one of many extant clues to the element of mystery in Beckett's work.

Paul Klee was probably the first to have said that art does not copy the visible, it makes visible. What Beckett is trying to express in words is so delicate that it may well appear that the author is making it difficult for his readers, perhaps more difficult than necessary. But this is not so. Beckett has defined it as his task to create a poetry "which has passed through nothingness" and which attempts a new beginning on the other side. It is a matter of indifference to him, as he once said, whether anyone cares to follow him there or not.[69]

67. Ibid., p. 20.
68. Cf. n. 52.
69. The following quotation is alleged to be by Beckett (without indication of the source): "For me the theater is not a moral institution in Schiller's

In view of this situation, it would be superficial to think that the "esoteric element," the mystery, is the result of Beckett's effort to disconcert or intentionally mislead the reader, that is, that the author wants to create total obscurity. The opposite is the case. Difficulties in the text can always be attributed to the nature of the object. Beckett cannot make the way any smoother than it actually is. To this extent it is impossible for him to spare the reader anything. None of the seemingly endless passages, none of the games of confusion (which often enough have only the semblance of logic), none of the series or enumerations can be omitted.

To put it another way, Beckett's texts correspond to an inner necessity and are not intended to make things appear more complicated, more puzzling, more "esoteric" to the reader than they really are. For Beckett there is no such thing as esotericism in the sense of an intentional obfuscation of what is actually meant. The more difficult the "object" of interest is to understand, the more sharply one's sight must be focused, that is, the clearer one's initial perception must be, and the more accurately that perception must be expressed in words. The first problem is developing the capacity to perceive, that is, a matter of sensibility, and the second is finding adequate means of expression. The esoteric element has to do with that which is to be perceived.

If it is valid to say that *Watt* represents an epistemological problem worth solving, then following Watt's development in the novel will necessarily lead us to the very set of hidden relationships which we have called esoteric. It must be possible to derive these relationships from the text and

---

sense. It is not my desire to teach or to improve or to help people pass the time. I want to bring poetry into drama, a poetry which has passed through nothingness and has found a new beginning in a new realm. I think in new dimensions, and basically it is of no concern to me who can follow. I have not been able to provide the answers which people wanted from me. There are no automatic solutions" (*Spektakulum* 6 [1963]: 319; original in German). Beckett's remarks to me in Berlin on September 9, 1967 were along exactly the same lines.

to understand them. The esoteric quality of a literary work cannot be of such a nature that it is impenetrable to serious analysis. More important than conceptual clarification or the definition of an underlying esoteric structure, however, is the process of understanding itself which the reader must undergo. It is comparable to the path of initiation which the disciples of the Greek mysteries were compelled to follow, for the goal is not simply to supply a more or less plausible psychological interpretation of *Watt* (of whatever sort), nor to substitute a mere explanation for an experience which can have real meaning only to the person who has lived through it. No interpretation, no matter how subtle, can be a substitute for following the same paths—esoteric paths—that Watt has traveled before us. Although the "disciple" recreates certain conceptual patterns in order to experience reality in a new way, the important thing is not the goal, but rather the personal effort required to achieve the goal.

Gotthold Ephraim Lessing has described the situation meant here. We should accept his choice as the only one worthy of human beings: "If God held all truth closed in his right hand, and if, closed in his left, he held the single, ever-burning need for truth, even though this would always and forever lead me astray, and if he were to say to me, 'Choose!' I would humbly take his left and say, 'Father, give me this. Pure truth can only be for you alone.' "[70] In other words, because man is not in possession of the truth, his real vocation is to strive to attain it.

If the assumption is valid that there is an esoteric content in *Watt* and that Watt's development can be understood only gradually by means of inner effort, then it is justifiable to use the term "gnosiological," rather than the more abstract and impersonal word "epistemological." My intention is to understand Beckett's novel in terms of its inner value, that is, existentially. This requires a vital and expandable capacity for

---

70. "Eine Duplik," in *Lessing Werke,* Schriften II, vol. 3 (Frankfurt am Main, 1967), p. 321.

understanding which can more easily adapt to the inner mental-spiritual reality described than the conventional methods of literary criticism with its fixed vocabulary and nailed down concepts.

The original concept of *gnosis*, from which "gnosiological" is derived, signifies quite specific contexts of knowledge, which will be referred to later (see chapter 4, pp. 154ff.). In Greece, the concept of *pistis* (faith) was the opposite of gnosis. We cannot discuss here the subsequent religious controversy which dominated early Christianity up to the condemnation—unnecessarily harsh to our modern way of thinking—of the gnostics as heretics. But I see no justification for a negative attitude toward the concept of gnosis on the basis of a long-past struggle in church history. In my opinion, the strict separation between knowledge and faith (the gnosis and pistis of the Greeks), which has been accepted since Kant, is not final. It is at least conceivable that the borderline between that which can be known and that which must (or should) be believed can shift as a result of an expansion in the realm of experience.

The term "gnosiological" itself was recommended to me by Beckett. In my book *Absurdes Theater und Bewusstseinswandel* (Theater of the Absurd and Man's Changing Consciousness),[71] which is dedicated to him, there is a chapter entitled "Beckett und die erkenntnistheoretische Grundsituation unserer Zeit" (Beckett and the Underlying Epistemological Situation of Our Time). Beckett had read this book when I visited him in Ussy on April 12, 1969, and we spoke of the possibility of a translation into English. Beckett suggested "epistemological" or "gnosiological" as possible English terms; the two are used synonymously today. He preferred the latter term, although the more common translation of the rather abstract-sounding *erkenntnistheoretisch* is "epistemological." Shortly thereafter I repeated my question on this point in writing in order to be quite sure what he had meant, whereupon Beckett

71. Berlin, 1968.

confirmed to me on May 31, 1969: " 'Epistemological' or 'Gnosiological,' but I think preferably the latter."[72]

Beckett's suggestion was therefore the deciding factor in the choice of this word for the formulation of my project. The adjective "gnosiological" thus serves to describe the theme of this study more precisely in that it is also my intention to find the most effective way to deal theoretically with Beckett's esoteric world. But it is also true that, since literature is involved and not just philosophy, my work concerns both theoretical knowledge *and* practical knowledge, in the sense of an expansion of the limits of experience.

Because *Watt* is definitely not just a mad, comical book dominated by parody, and not merely a depiction of the desolate state in which man finds himself in our modern alienated world (a view which many others share besides Beckett), a starting point had to be found which does justice not only to the philosophy of the author but also to his whole attitude toward the process of artistic creation. Only after the esoteric content of *Watt* has been illuminated gnosiologically to satisfy these conditions will it be possible to give the novel its proper place in the canon of Beckett's complete works, a place it has not yet been given.

It will still be difficult, because of the problems discussed above, to penetrate to the core of *Watt*, but this difficulty is inherent in the novel itself. A number of layers will have to be removed step by step; although these are obviously part of the whole, they still function like the peel around a fruit. Chapters 2 and 3 serve the purpose of peeling away these outer layers.

72. Facsimile of the passage from the letter:

Procedure

Chapter 2 deals with the events described by Beckett in *Watt;* that is, it summarizes the events of the novel with respect to its gnosiological content.

Chapter 3 is devoted to the composition of the novel. An evaluation of the various critical debates is intentionally omitted so that the meaning of the compositional elements can be analyzed. As the review of the secondary literature has shown, there are several important studies of *Watt* which pertain to the structure of the novel, its various narrative points of view, and so forth.

Chapter 4 presents a discussion of the underlying gnosiological aspect of *Watt* as it has been revealed by the close reading of the text.

Other works by Beckett will be cited to the extent required for an understanding of *Watt* (as a novel) and of Watt (as a character). The process of comparison, focusing on meaning, will define the scope and limits of this procedure. It is obvious that, when appropriate, other Beckett scholars will be allowed to speak. In addition to use of the technique of comparison in order to objectify, I also make use of empathetic, contemplative re-creation in the sense defined in the previous section of chapter 1. Only in this way can the gnosiological content of *Watt* be uncovered; only in this way can the new which Beckett has embodied in this novel be revealed through his inner approach to the so-called "nothingness."

The Content of the Novel Watt

I am Watt, said Watt. As you say, I'm unrecogni-
zable. Watt? said Camier. The name means nothing
to me. I am not widely known, said Watt, but I shall
be, one day.
    Mercier and Camier[73]

II

73. Samuel Beckett, *Mercier and Camier* (London, 1974; New York, 1975), p. 111.

In spite of the intrinsic deficiencies of a plot summary, the sequence of events in the novel is described below with the help of quotations from the text. This will provide an opportunity to emphasize certain elements which are important to the argument. Only someone intimate with the book will be able to follow this precis without a sense of impoverishment, for a summary of any sort destroys the essential totality of a work of art. Despite these objections, two reasons motivate me to paraphrase the content of *Watt*. First, it can be shown that, in contrast to the opinion of other critics, there is a continuous story line, even though there are frequent lapses from traditional narrative structure. Second, many notable Beckett scholars have analyzed *Watt* without devoting any attention to the special aspect forming the object of this study which is referred to generally as its gnosiological aspect.

Part I: Introductory Events and Watt's Journey to Mr. Knott's House

Watt begins with a narrative frame which attunes the reader to the theme of the novel as a whole. A certain Mr. Hackett, who makes no other appearance in the book, turns a corner and sees "his" seat. By turning this corner with Mr. Hackett, we also enter the scene of the action. This Mr. Hackett is a short, hunched man, who advances laboriously with a cane in his right hand while supporting himself with his left on the bars of a railing.

After a lengthy discussion of such perennial themes as love, pregnancy, and birth, we finally learn that Mr. Hackett is hunchbacked because of a fall from a ladder at one year of age while abandoned by his mother (who was "out somewhere") and his father (who was in the mountains "breaking stones"). Only a goat is said to have been with the child. The story of the abandoned child, later the crippled Mr. Hackett, is very sad. His faithless mother is the subject of the following remarks:

> And what possessed her to slip off like that? said Goff.
>
> I never asked her, said Mr Hackett. The pub, or the chapel, or both.
>
> Poor woman, God forgive her, said Tetty.
>
> Faith I wouldn't put it past him, said Mr Hackett.
>
> (P. 16)

This passage is characteristic of Beckett's sarcastic humor.

This is the situation when Watt enters. A tram stops, and after it has moved on again Watt is standing on the opposite side of the street.

These preliminaries can be considered a narrative frame. The figure of Watt appears on page 16, and by page 24 the other figures have disappeared, having fulfilled their function. Watt is first presented indirectly, as seen by the secondary characters who have been observing him.

Mr. Hackett and the farcical pair, Goff and Tetty Nixon, have not been introduced, however, just to observe Watt and animate a certain locality—the bench at the tram stop. What is involved here is already part of the basic theme of the entire book: the process of being born (as a result of dubious interpersonal relationships) into a definitely "hunchbacked" world.

A similar narrative frame is found again toward the end of the novel, but not with the same secondary characters. When at the end Watt returns to the train station, where he spends the night, the characters who observe him and comment on the events are railway employees and travelers.

Mr. Hackett suspects that Watt has made a mistake in getting off the tram here; after all, he had wanted to go to the train station. It is apparent also that Watt is afraid—afraid of burdening himself with the onus of a decision. Mr. Hackett also suspects that Watt finds the thought of leaving the city as painful as the thought of remaining in it, and that therefore he has left the decision "to the frigid machinery of the time-space relation" (p. 21), that is, he leaves whether or not he will miss the train to chance.

It can be seen that Watt is wearing a hat on his head, but Mr. Nixon professes to know nothing about his nationality, family, place of birth, religion, profession, income, or identifying characteristics. This prompts Mr. Hackett to expostulate, "One does not part with five shillings to a shadow" (p. 21).

Mr. Nixon finally admits that he had once met Watt on the street, at which time Watt had had one bare foot, that Watt is most probably a university man, and that he still drinks only milk. Watt appears to have borrowed five shillings from Mr. Nixon to buy a shoe for his bare foot. Mr. and Mrs. Nixon go off arm in arm while Mr. Hackett remains sitting in pitch darkness.

With this we leave Mr. Hackett. The framing introduction is over, and our interest is directed to Watt, who in the meantime has apparently arrived at the station platform.

Watt's journey is now described without digression. He collides with a porter on the platform, whose milk can is almost tipped over. Watt stands up again, little the worse for wear. The porter curses, "The devil raise a hump on you" (p. 24), which would, of course, make Watt resemble Mr. Hackett, although this is only suggested.

Watt lets the remark pass, and although he wants to pick up his hat and bags again, he simply folds his hands and "smiles." To many of the bystanders, however, this smile looks more like "a simple sucking of the teeth."

We see Watt at the beginning of his journey, therefore, with his hands folded on his chest and an expression on his face suggestive of toothless gums. And although this remarkable entry of Watt is explicitly referred to as "an incident . . . of too common a kind" to provoke interest, there were nevertheless present "connoisseurs on whom the exceptional quality of Watt was not lost" (p. 25).

Watt finally picks up his bags and climbs into the train. He sits facing the rear. "Already Watt preferred to have his back to his destination" (p. 26). He thus prefers not to see what is coming or where his journey is taking him.

There follows an encounter with the editor of a Catholic monthly magazine, a Mr. Spiro, who is sitting opposite Watt (i.e., facing forward). Mr. Spiro claims, "We keep our tonsure above water" (p. 27), and provides examples of the pious sophistries used to entertain his readers.

Watt must be ready to leave the train as soon as it stops. Because there are only a few passengers on this line, the train barely pauses before it moves on again. There is no explicit mention of Watt's leaving the train. While Mr. Spiro continues to travel through the night alone with his problems, Watt begins straightway to struggle on foot through the darkness, which, to be sure, is lit by an unpleasantly yellow moon. Watt's gait is described as a "funambulistic stagger." He throws himself stiff-legged from one side to the other without bending his knees. His feet land flat on the ground and leave it "for the air's uncharted ways, with manifest repugnancy" (p. 31). This is indeed a remarkable way of achieving forward motion.

Weakness overcomes Watt and he sits down for a time on the path at the side of the road, his hat pushed back, his bags next to him, his knees drawn up, his arms on his knees, and his head on his arms—"The parts of the body are really very friendly at such times" (p. 33). Soon he stretches out and listens to the sounds of the night, half on the road, half on the path at the edge of a ditch. Finally he rolls himself over into the ditch, where he lies,

> on his face, half buried in the wild long grass, the foxgloves, the hyssop, the pretty nettles, the high pouting hemlock, and other ditch weeds and flowers. (P. 33)

Now Watt hears what sounds like a grotesque "chorus of angels":[74]

> And it was to him lying thus that there came, with great distinctness, from afar, from without, yes, really it seemed from without, the voices, indifferent in quality, of a mixed choir. (P. 33)

It was stated earlier that Watt could not abide two things, the moon and the sun, but now it seems that it is the earth and the sky which are loathsome to him. So Watt crawls out of the ditch, not forgetting his bags, and resumes his journey "with less difficulty than he had feared" (p. 36) because he has left both his weakness and his dinner (of goat's milk and insufficiently cooked cod) behind in the ditch.

> It was with confidence that he now advanced, in the middle of the road, with confidence and with awe also, for the chimneys of Mr Knott's house were visible at last, in the light, of the moon. (P. 36)

Arriving at Mr. Knott's house, Watt finds the front door locked and so goes to the back door, but this is also closed. He circles the house and, after finding the front door still closed, suddenly finds the back door open so that he can enter. Watt is surprised to find himself inside and has no idea how he actually entered.

> Two explanations of this occurred to him. The first was this, that his science of the locked door, so seldom at

---

74. See Senneff, "Song and Music," pp. 137–49; and Warhaft, "Threne and Theme in *Watt*," pp. 261–78. In spite of the importance the two authors give this threne, the music and text are reproduced only in the original edition. In the German and French versions, Beckett is content to refer to this mixed chorus, together with the footnote also present in the original: "What, it may be enquired, was the music of this threne? What at least, it may be demanded, did the soprano sing?" (*Watt*, p. 33)

fault, had been so on this occasion, and that the back door, when he had found it locked, had not been locked, but open. (P. 36)

The second possibility was that someone had opened it from the inside or from the outside, "while he Watt had been employed in going to and fro." Watt is forced to prefer the latter explanation "as being the more beautiful" (p. 36). The fact remains, however, that Watt does not really know how he entered Mr. Knott's house, that is, how he was actually able to cross the threshold.

Almost as soon as Watt enters, he realizes that the house is not so dark as he originally thought. He sits down in the kitchen next to the light and watches the ashes as they turn gray in the grate. He takes off his hat (revealing tufts of red-gray hair) and puts down his bags, for he has reached his destination.

Watt now busies himself covering and uncovering the lamp with his hat so that he can see the fire, which is almost out, turn red, then turn gray, and then turn red again. He is so occupied that he neither sees nor hears the door open and a man enter. It is Arsene, the departing servant of Mr. Knott, who in the following pages presents Watt with a "short statement" which is intended to acquaint him with what he is to expect at Mr. Knott's house.

ARSENE'S STATEMENT

Arsene first claims that the travels of all those eventually arriving at Mr. Knott's house have not been aimless. "For one is come, to stay. Haw! All the old ways led to this, all the old windings" (p. 40). Then Arsene gives Watt a preview of what awaits him.

The change associated with entry into Mr. Knott's house is radical, as if one has been transported to a foreign country. And it happens quickly—"What was changed was existence off the ladder" (p. 44). But what is the reality, if any at all, to which this sudden, nongradual, radical change corresponds?

Whatever it is, Arsene states expressly that everyone winds up sooner or later in this same situation, "for in truth the same things happen to us all . . . if only we chose to know it" (p. 45). After a reflection on the passage of time and death, life on earth is termed in general "an ordure, from beginning to end" (p. 46). This is underscored in the form of the first "series" or enumeration:

> Not a word, not a deed, not a thought, not a need . . . And the poor old lousy old earth, my earth and my father's and my mother's and my father's father's . . . the whole bloody business starting all over again. A turd. And if I could begin it all over again, knowing what I know now, the result would be the same . . . And if I could begin it all over again a hundred times, knowing each time a little more than the time before, the result would always be the same, and the hundredth life as the first, and the hundred lives as one. (Pp. 46–47)

The generations and then the seasons are treated in this way, the whole miserable story, and the conclusion is—"a turd." Observation of life reveals it to be a vale of tears. Arsene's laughter, which could be more accurately described as an Indian's howl, has three components: it is bitter, hollow, and mirthless, corresponding to "excoriations of the understanding" (p. 48).

The prospect of now having to leave Mr. Knott's house plunges Arsene into profound sorrow. He sees that he will return to the same misery as before and is so sad that only the thought of death remains, "the feeling of sorrow, sorrow for what has been, is and is to come" (p. 49). But Arsene will leave Watt in his place,

> with before you all I have behind me, and all I have before me . . . for the coming is in the shadow of the going and the going is in the shadow of the coming . . . (Pp. 56–57)

Arsene goes, but when he came, Vincent left, and Walter left when Erskine came. The sequence obeys one of the rules of the house, that there are always two servants. When one ascends to the upper floor, the servant who has been working there until then can go, while the new man begins his service on the ground floor. This game is a "come and go" according to fixed rules; it thus recalls the play by Beckett of the same name. "And yet there is one who neither comes nor goes, I refer I need hardly say to my late employer" (p. 57). Those who come and go "nest a little while in his branches" (p. 57), says Arsene, introducing a metaphor for Mr. Knott which returns in part III of *Watt*. What is the point of this coming and going? What is the meaning of being there? Arsene's answer is:

> And though in purposelessness I may seem now to go, yet I do not, any more than in purposelessness then I came, for I go now with my purpose as with it then I came, the only difference being this, that then it was living and now it is dead. (P. 58)

Mr. Knott is surrounded by servants, all of whom are imperfect in some way. They are either little, fat, shabby, and seedy men, or big, bony, shabby, seedy, haggard, and knock-kneed men. The list is endless and its beginning is lost in time,

> until all trace is lost, owing to the shortness of human memory, one always ousting the other, though perhaps ousting is not the word . . . (P. 60)

> And I think I have said enough to light that fire in your mind that shall never be snuffed, or only with the utmost difficulty. (P. 62)

Arsene concludes at last, "Not that I have told you all I

know, for I have not" (p. 62), for ultimately the attempt to convey the full extent of his knowledge can only fail

> because what we know partakes in no small measure of the nature of what has so happily been called the unutterable or ineffable, so that any attempt to utter or eff it is doomed to fail, doomed, doomed to fail. (P. 62)

Watt must make the rest of the journey himself, initially with Erskine at his side, whose responsibilities are now on the upper floor, and then for the rest, alone,

> or only with shades to keep you company, and that I think you will find, if your experience at all resembles mine, the best part of the outing. (P. 63)

Finally Arsene begs to be forgiven for all that he has said, "with forgiveness, as you desire to be thought of" (p. 63).

At the end of this first part of *Watt*, Arsene stands on the threshold, his gaze directed at Watt, and disappears, "by a firm unhurried hand, wiped away" (p. 64). Watt sees the sky turn gray. Light would come, gradually, whether it suited him or not,

> all the unsoiled light of the new day, of the new day at last, the day without precedent at last. (P. 64)

Part II: Watt's Experiences on the Ground Floor of Mr. Knott's House

"Mr Knott was a good master, in a way," Watt says to himself. This remark introduces Watt's report on his period of residence on the ground floor of Mr. Knott's house. It is conspicuous here that Mr. Knott is referred to as "master." There is always a certain distance between Mr. Knott and those around him. A strict hierarchy is in force. Even the upper floor slops are not disposed of there. Rather, they are brought down by Erskine to be spread out by Watt in the garden as fertilizer. Watt believes that this is perhaps not the real reason, but only the reason offered to the understanding. This implies, of course, that there are other reasons for Mr. Knott's instructions which are not accessible to the understanding.

Mr. Knott never leaves his property, at least as far as Watt can judge. Watt does not think it possible that this could occur without his knowledge. Only once do strangers ever cross the threshold during this period. This is when the Galls, father and son, arrive to tune the piano. The elder Gall is blind (as are many piano tuners), so that the son must lead him by the arm. It is expressly stated that there is no family resemblance of any kind between them.

> How very fortunate for Mr Gall, said Watt, that he has his son at his command, whose manner is all devotion. (P. 71)

It is therefore surprising that it is the younger Gall who tunes the piano, even though the piano has been completely destroyed by mice.

> The piano is doomed, in my opinion, said the younger.
> The piano-tuner also, said the elder.
> The pianist also, said the younger. (P. 72)

It turns out that this is "perhaps the principal incident of Watt's early days in Mr Knott's house," and it repeats or propagates itself in Watt's mind. Insofar as such an event offers only material for reflection or serves merely as an example of something, it is the starting point for a potentially endless series of transformations in meaning.

> This fragility of the outer meaning had a bad effect on Watt, for it caused him to seek for another, for some

meaning of what had passed, in the image of how it had passed. (P. 73)

Watt takes this opportunity to reflect on the difference between what has happened and *how* it has happened, that is, on the image which the event causes in the mind, because an image is never just an image but is always a reference to something else as well.

Other incidents follow the visit from the Galls, incidents similar in that they are "of great formal brilliance and indeterminable purport" (p. 74). It is clear that Watt's description of his experiences has become problematic:

> Watt could not accept them for what they perhaps were, the simple games that time plays with space, . . . but was obliged, because of his peculiar character, to enquire into what they meant, . . . into what they might be induced to mean, with the help of a little patience, a little ingenuity. (P. 75)

One of the problems is that the recorder of Watt's experiences learns of them only after they have receded into the past. There is also the difficulty of not being able to understand Watt clearly because of the rapidity of his speech and the peculiarities of his syntax.

Watt has had to learn to live with these incidents, which are not so much concrete events as they are "apparitions," the term used in the French edition of *Watt* for the rare occasions when Mr. Knott is seen (on his way from the second floor to the garden). Because the events are transitory, and because they have the character of images, it is necessary for Watt to make a continuing effort to understand them.

The state in which Watt now finds himself is more inaccessible to description than any in which he has ever been before. Therefore, in an effort to learn what Erskine, the other servant, cannot tell him (that is, what words are to be applied to the "conditions of being" in which Erskine finds himself), Watt tries to figure out what Arsene had attempted to convey by his parting "statement," for the objects around him resist naming. A pot is not just a pot, no matter how closely it might resemble one:

> It was vain that it answered, with unexceptionable adequacy, all the purposes, and performed all the offices, of a pot, it was not a pot. And it was just this hairbreadth departure from the nature of a true pot that so excruciated Watt. (P. 81)

Watt actually prefers to deal with things whose names he does not know, even though this is also painful. He needs to name what he sees:

> Watt's need of semantic succour was at times so great that he would set to trying names on things. (P. 83)

There are also times in which Watt feels a certain satisfaction in his loneliness, a certain pleasure in noting that the "last rats" have abandoned him. The possible meaning of the rat symbol will be discussed in chapter 4.

In the first weeks of his stay, Watt still had words at his disposal: "Watt's words had not yet begun to fail him, or Watt's world to become unspeakable" (p. 85). Watt appears to become more and more inwardly estranged from the world he lived in before coming to Mr. Knott's house. Finally, he no longer needs Erskine's questions, no longer requires confirmation through his voice.

> But he would have appreciated it more if it had come earlier, before he had grown used to his loss of species . . .
>
> Watt's attention was extreme, in the beginning, to all that went on about him. (P. 85)

Watt obviously makes an effort to orient himself in his new environment:

> This constant tension of some of his most noble faculties tired Watt greatly. And the results, on the whole, were meagre. (P. 86)

The reference to sense perceptions in this, to Watt, new realm, is worthy of note. We will return to it in chapter 4.

After Watt has become accustomed to life in Mr. Knott's house and to the rules by which it is run, the story turns to Mr. Knott and his habits, presenting us with a series of grotesque descriptions of his food, his eating habits, and the disposal of his leftovers. These passages are quite comical. Mr. Knott's food is an improbable mixture of all possible types of edible substances and ingredients, including several items solely for the good of the health. All this is thoroughly mixed in the famous pot and cooked for four hours until it achieves the consistency of "a mess, or poss." These good things to eat, drink, and promote the health are so inextricably combined that a new, single good thing is created, even one spoonful of which is sufficient to stimulate and destroy the appetite simultaneously.

Watt is obliged to weigh, measure, and count all the ingredients accurately and to mix and cook them. This job calls upon all of Watt's powers, those of his spirit and his body, to the point at which he must shed "tears of mental fatigue," which also fall into the pot. This dish is prepared to provide fourteen servings, seven full luncheons and seven full dinners. Mr. Knott eats them cold at all times, in a bowl, punctually at twelve and seven. Watt must place the bowl in the dining room and retrieve it an hour later. If the bowl still contains food it is carried to the dog's trough, but if it is empty Watt washes it out. Mr. Knott is never heard to complain about his food, although he does not always eat it.

WATT'S CURIOSITY ABOUT ERSKINE'S RESPONSIBILITIES

Occasionally Mr. Knott rings in the night. Although the bell is in Erskine's room, its sound, or the sound of Erskine getting up and going down, prevents Watt from sleeping soundly at night. Watt asks himself whether Erskine is quite sane, or whether he himself might not be a bit deranged:

> And Mr Knott himself, was he quite right in his head? Were they not all three perhaps a little off the hooks? (P. 122)

It remains unclear to Watt who it is that actually rings. Perhaps Erskine himself does. As a last resort, Watt decides to inspect Erskine's room (which is on the third floor), but his room is always locked.

> The lock was of a kind that Watt could not pick. Watt could pick simple locks, but he could not pick obscure locks . . .
> Then Watt said, Obscure keys may open simple locks, but simple keys obscure locks never. But Watt had hardly said this when he regretted having done so. But then it was too late, the words were said and could never be forgotten, never undone. But a little later he regretted them less. And a little later he did not regret them at all. (P. 124)

The narrator thus describes how Watt vacillates in his attitude toward the words which were somehow spoken; he then informs us that everything he has to tell us originates from Watt himself:

> For all that I know on the subject of Mr Knott, and of all that touched Mr Knott, and on the subject of Watt, and of all that touched Watt, came from Watt, and from Watt alone. (P. 125)

But apart from this, it is difficult for a man like Watt to tell a long story like Watt's without leaving out some things, and foisting in others. (P. 126)

The narrator, who thus suddenly identifies himself here, insists that he has made an all-out effort to record everything immediately to guarantee the accuracy of his report.

Watt persists in his desire to know what is going on in Erskine's room. In order to get in, Watt would have to become "another man"—or Erskine's room another room. Nothing changes, yet Watt manages to get inside Erskine's room by a ruse. This ruse consists in his beginning to think or to speak backwards, to stand things on their head, so to speak. We encounter this "ruse" again in part III of the novel to a fuller extent. In this way Watt's success in penetrating Erskine's world here for the first time foreshadows his own later realm of existence.

Although Watt finds the bell in Erskine's room, as he suspected he would, the bell is broken. A remarkable painting is hanging on the wall, and it is described minutely. It shows a circular black line, which is broken at its lowest point (the nadir). On the right side in the background is a blue dot or point.

> By what means the illusion of movement in space, and it almost seemed in time, was given, Watt could not say. But it was given. (Pp. 128–29)

Watt wonders what the artist had wanted to show:

> At the thought that it was perhaps this, a circle and a centre not its centre in search of a centre and its circle respectively, in boundless space, in endless time, then Watt's eyes filled with tears . . . (P. 129)

> It is by the nadir that we come, said Watt, and it is by the nadir that we go, whatever that means. (P. 130)

It is thus suggested that to enter or to leave Mr. Knott's world it is necessary to pass through some form of "nadir."

After these tedious deliberations, Watt comes to the conclusion that the painting must be an integral component of Mr. Knott's household. He also notices that nothing can be added or taken away from the house—everything is just as it was at the beginning and as it ever shall be. Only external appearances change in this state of the eternal present:

> Nothing changed, in Mr Knott's establishment, because nothing remained, and nothing came or went, because all was a coming and a going.
>
> Watt seemed highly pleased with this tenth rate xenia. Spoken as he spoke it, back to front, it has a certain air, it is true. (Pp. 131–32)

Watt's time on the ground floor of the house approaches its end, but he has lost his awareness of the passage of time:

> As it turned out, Watt was never to know how long he spent in Mr Knott's house, how long on the ground floor, how long on the first floor, how long altogether. All he could say was that it seemed a long time. (P. 136)*

Until now, Watt has had only rare glimpses of Mr. Knott:

> Sometimes in the vestibule Watt would catch a glimpse of Mr Knott, or in the garden . . . (P. 145)

> Watt did not know whether he was glad or sorry that he did not see Mr Knott more often . . . Yes indeed, in so far as he wished, in so far as he feared, to see Mr Knott face to face, his wish made him sorry, his fear glad, that he saw him so seldom. (P. 146)

As hope and fear recede little by little, Watt's interest in the essence of Mr. Knott increases and his interest in what is

---

*Editor's note: The "ground floor" and "first floor" in this passage and throughout *Watt* itself are, in American usage, the first and second floors.

usually thought of as the body decreases. Furthermore, the form which Watt perceives as Mr. Knott is constantly changing; he rarely if ever sees the same figure twice.

Watt is now tired of being on the ground floor:

> What had he learnt? Nothing.
> What did he know of Mr Knott? Nothing.
> Of his anxiety to improve, of his anxiety to understand, of his anxiety to get well, what remained? Nothing.
> But was not that something? (P. 148)

These references to "nothing" echo the words of Democritus quoted by Beckett in *Malone Dies:* "Nothing is more real than nothing" (p. 193). This statement, which at first glance appears devoid of meaning, can be considered a key to Beckett's work. This opinion is shared by Richard W. Seaver.[75]

Part II concludes with a lyrical description of the day on which Watt arises and notices that Erskine has departed. When Watt comes into the kitchen he finds the new man sitting there. The man says his name is Arthur, and he resembles Arsene and Erskine in physical appearance.

Part III: Watt's Experiences on the Second Floor— Watt and Sam

The chief ideas of the third part of *Watt* are even more difficult to define than those of the preceding part. Anyone who has come this far probably expects now to find Watt on the second floor of Mr. Knott's house in Erskine's place, but the content and character of the descriptions initially appear to disappoint this expectation.

Part III begins with the words, "It was about this time that Watt was transferred to another pavilion, leaving me be-

75. Seaver, ed., *I can't go on, I'll go on: A Selection from Samuel Beckett's Work* (New York, 1976).

hind in the old pavilion" (p. 149). This beginning and a number of points which follow have created the suspicion that
Watt is a mental patient in an insane asylum. There is in fact
much evidence to support this view. Psychiatric institutions
frequently consist of a number of separate buildings, often
called pavilions. In addition, such phrases as "looking about
me, like a mad creature" (p. 158) and "continuing my inspection, like one deprived of his senses" (p. 159) also support
this suspicion.

It is questionable, however, whether such externals are
a firm enough basis for concluding that the entire story occurs
in an insane asylum.[76] Even if the action creates the impression that madness reigns and that the imagination is out of
control, there can be other reasons for this. In purely formal
terms, it is enough to see the beginning of a new narrative
point of view here. What is particularly striking in this first
sentence is that Watt's ascent to the next higher floor—already
prepared for in part II—is associated with an apparent split
into Watt and a "narrator." This narrator speaks in the first
person and surprises us by introducing himself as "Sam."

It is as if Sam has emerged from Watt or Watt from Sam.
This interpretation, which explains the sudden appearance of
Sam, is more informative than the rather theoretical notion
that Sam must have already been functioning as the narrator,
even though he is not identified until this point. There is no
apparent reason for such a delay. Although this interpretation
of Sam is conceivable, in view of Beckett's direct narrative
style it is not convincing. At the very least we can say that if
Sam had been necessary earlier, Beckett would have introduced him by name.

76. Many critics share this opinion. Alfred Alvarez also thinks he notices "signs of psychosis," which give the work its never quite silent undertone of doom and catastrophe (*Beckett* [London, 1978]). Rolf Breuer (*Die Kunst
der Paradoxie*, p. 48) and Horst Breuer (*Samuel Beckett*, p. 157) also suspect
schizophrenia. Russell Mears has written about this in "Beckett, Sarraute,
and the Perceptual Experience of Schizophrenia," *Psychiatry*, no. 36 (1973),
pp. 61–69.

Another argument against linking the term *pavilion* exclusively with an insane asylum is that the word is used loosely. The term *mansion* is used in the English version (*Zwinger* in the German edition) on the very first page of part III, whereas the French edition retains *pavillon,* the term used initially in all three languages.

There must be both sun and wind if Sam and Watt are to meet outdoors; otherwise they prefer to remain in their houses, "each in his separate soundless unlit warmth":

> For when on Sam the sun shone bright, then in a vacuum panted Watt, and when Watt like a leaf was tossed, then stumbled Sam in deepest night. But ah, when exceptionally the desired degrees of ventilation and radiance were united, in the little garden, then we were peers in peace, each in his own way, until the wind fell, the sun declined. (P. 153)

Watt and Sam repair a bridge, lying on their stomachs, each from his own side; they are thus not on the same side of the stream. After they have completed their work, they smile at each other with an "exceptional smile," for they are happy at having established the connection. There are no benches on which they can rest. Thickets, brakes, and brambles abound, and there are many birds, which the two companions delight in pursuing with stones. Their particular friends are the rats, which live on the banks of the stream. Watt and Sam feed them with tidbits from their "ordinary" or even feed one rat to another. This occasions the unusual remark that they feel they have come "nearest to God" while engaged in these activities. Watt speaks with a low, rapid voice, which makes it difficult to understand him correctly, and he does not pay much regard to the rules of grammar. Much of what he says is lost forever in the rushing wind.

There are in fact many other gardens, all surrounded by high barbed wire fences greatly in need of repair. This reinforces the impression that we are in an insane asylum.

One day Sam is driven to the fence "as though by some external agency," in the brilliant sun and tempestuous wind. Sam loves the fences; even though they limit motion, they do not limit vision. Watt has a similar attitude. Thus a remarkable meeting occurs:

> Being now so near the fence, that I could have touched it with a stick, if I had wished, and so looking about me, like a mad creature, I perceived, beyond all possibility of error, that I was in the presence of one of those channels or straits described above, where the limit of my garden, and that of another, followed the same course, at so short a remove, the one from the other, and for so considerable a distance, that it was impossible for doubts not to arise, in a reasonable mind, regarding the sanity of the person responsible for the lay-out. Continuing my inspection, like one deprived of his senses, I observed, with a distinctness that left no room for doubt, in the adjoining garden whom do you think but Watt. (Pp. 158–59)

In what follows, everything occurs backward. First Watt, who approaches the fence slowly and deviously, is walking backward toward Sam. But he also speaks in sentences in which the individual words are in reverse order. Sam cries,

> Why, Watt, . . . that is a nice state you have got yourself into, to be sure. Not it is, yes, replied Watt. [That is, "Yes, is it not?"] (P. 159)

Watt has crept backward through the brambles, the briars, and the thistles and has reached the barbed wire, where he now hangs with outstretched arms. "His face was bloody, his hands also, and thorns were in his scalp" (p. 159). Watt thus resembles the portrait of Christ attributed to Bosch that was at that time hanging in the National Gallery on

Trafalgar Square, as is noted in the text in parentheses. Watt stammers:

> Wonder I, said Watt, panky-hanky me lend you could, blood away wipe. [Translated: "I wonder, said Watt, could you lend me hanky-panky, wipe away blood."] (Pp. 159–60)

Sam attempts to give Watt the handkerchief through a hole in the fence but cannot locate him. Watt has been relieving himself in the bushes and reveals not only that he now walks and talks in reverse, but also that he has his pants on backwards.

Sam finally is able to pull Watt over to his side of the fence through the hole. He wipes Watt's face and hands, rubs some ointment on him, combs his tufts of hair and sideburns, brushes off his clothing, and finally turns him around so that they are standing face to face. "Then I placed his hands, on my shoulders, his left hand on my right shoulder . . ." (p. 163). They walk along together in this way, Sam forward, Watt backward, between the fences,

> I looking whither we were going, and he looking whence we were coming. (P. 163)

> So we began, after so long a time, to walk together again, and to talk . . .
> As Watt walked, so now he talked, back to front. (P. 164)

It is important for an understanding of the text that follows to point out that Sam and Watt continue together in this way, Sam walking forward, Watt walking (and talking) backward, until the end of part III, at which point we read:

> When he had told me this, then he loosed my hands from his shoulders, and backwards through the hole went back, to his garden, and left me alone. (P. 213)

What we read, however, from page 164 to the end of the chapter, are examples of the way in which Watt spoke at that time and of what Watt said to Sam in inversions that more or less completely recount what Watt experienced during the period in question. For Sam, whose primary concern is with "information," these inversions are quite confusing:

> Thus I missed I suppose much I presume of great interest touching I suspect the second stage of the second or closing period of Watt's stay in Mr Knott's house. (P. 165)

It is obvious from this sentence that all these descriptions are of Watt's experiences on the second floor of Mr. Knott's house, even though the appearances are at the first deceiving (see chapter 4, pp. 121ff.). They are illustrations of the various phases of consciousness through which Watt passes while in Mr. Knott's house. First he reverses the order of the words in the sentence, then the letters in the word, then the sentences in the paragraph, and so forth, until finally Watt's speech sounds like so much Irish to Sam:

> But soon I grew used to these sounds, and then I understood as well as ever, that is to say fully one half of what won its way past my tympan.
> For my own hearing now began to fail, though my myopia remained stationary. My purely mental faculties . . . were if possible more vigorous than ever. (P. 169)

There follows a scene in which "all four" are present in the garden: Mr. Knott, Watt, Arthur (Watt's successor on the ground floor), and Mr. Graves (the gardener). It remains unclear exactly where Sam is, but perhaps he has become so intermeshed with Watt that they count as one and the same person. Arthur tells a long story about his friend Ernest Louit and Mr. Thomas Nackybal; it is an unmistakable persiflage of the academic world. The exchange of glances among the individual members of an academic committee is not only comical but also utterly mad, and more than six full pages are required to describe the process. The following passage is inserted:

> For many, many looks may still be taken, and much, much time still lost, ere every eye find the eye it seeks, and into every mind the energy flow, the comfort and the reassurance, necessary for a resumption of the business in hand. And all this comes of lack of method. (P. 178)

A "garden series" follows, and finally the episode ends in a complete chaos of numbers and names, that is, in the irrational. This chaos is the result of the committee's "thorough examination" of Mr. Nackybal (also referred to once as "Ballynack"), from which he emerges with distinction.

Apparently Mr. Knott has climbed a tree, or disappeared from sight into the tree, while Arthur is telling this story. Furthermore,

> Watt learned later, from Arthur, that the telling of this story . . . had transported Arthur far from Mr Knott's premises. (P. 198)

It turns out that Arthur interrupts his story not because he is tired but because he wishes to return to Mr. Knott's house, to its mysteries and its fixity.

I see Arthur's story as the same type of retrospective view (of a previous life) that we encountered in Arsene's "statement" to Watt in which, just before his departure, Arsene looks back over his experiences in Mr. Knott's house. There is a striking contrast, however, between the second floor on which Mr. Knott lives and the world in which Arthur's story about Louit and Mr. Nackybal took place. Seen from Mr. Knott's point of view, that is, *sub specie eternita-*

tis, the doings described by Arthur, the newcomer, actually do seem quite absurd.

Watt himself has little to say about this second or final phase of his stay in Mr. Knott's house. He has learned little about his master, for the data available to his senses are scanty in the first place and they fade away quickly. Mr. Knott appears to move in a soundless void and an airless darkness. His clothing is undefinable and constantly changing—this is the basis for another "series." The anthropomorphism of these observations is obvious even to Watt. Watt is not a privileged initiate, but only an imperfect witness. All the same, in spite of the unintelligibility of his circumstances, Watt retains his peace of mind (ataraxy):

> This ataraxy covered the entire house-room, the pleasure-garden, the vegetable-garden and of course Arthur. (P. 208)

When the time has come for Watt to go, he proceeds to the gate in a state of utmost serenity, but after he has stepped into the public road he bursts into tears. He simply stands there, hanging his head, holding a bag in each hand.

At the end of part III it is mentioned that Watt and Sam part again, Watt walking backwards away from Sam to disappear through the hole in the fence to his own garden and pavilion. This is emphasized again on a symbolic level by the mixing and separating of smoke:

> And from the hidden pavilions, his and mine, where by this time dinner was preparing, the issuing smokes by the wind were blown, now far apart, but now together, mingled to vanish. (P. 213)

Part IV: Watt's Departure and Journey Back to the Railway Station

> As Watt told the beginning of his story, not first, but second, so not fourth, but third, now he told its end. Two, one, four, three, that was the order. (P. 215)

Part IV of *Watt* thus begins with a game of confusion. I discuss this structural peculiarity in chapter 3, pp. 84ff.). The narrative thread itself is picked up again with the words: "As Watt came, so he went, in the night" (p. 215).

It is summer again. Mr. Knott is in his room, and Watt is sitting at the open window, looking and listening. Arthur's step can be heard on the stairs, and the gleam of poor Arthur's light can be seen. Around midnight Watt helps Mr. Knott into his nightdress and into bed and then goes down to the kitchen for a last glass of milk. A stranger is sitting in the kitchen in the glow of the dying fire. It is Micks, who has entered the house the same way Watt managed to get in at first: "One moment I was out, and the next I was in" (p. 216). He is Arthur's successor on the ground floor, as Arthur is Watt's on the second floor. Thus Micks's arrival signals Watt's departure—everyone knows the rules.

The new man introduces himself:

> I come from — , said Mr Micks, and he described the place whence he came. I was born at — , he said, and the site and circumstances of his ejection were unfolded. My dear parents, he said, and Mr and Mrs Micks, heroic figures, unique in the annals of cloistered fornication, filled the kitchen. He said further, At the age of fifteen, My beloved wife, My beloved dog, Till at last. Happily Mr Micks was childless. (P. 216)

This aphoristic and completely contrary manner of introduction also requires an explanation, which will be provided later.

Then Micks, showing all the signs of horror, recoils to the wall, holding his hand in front of his face as if to ward off a blow. This is perplexing, because Micks was not an inexperienced person:

> Nor was Micks a little girl, or an innocent little choirboy, no, but a big placid man, who had seen something of the world. (P. 220)

Something has frightened and repelled him, "a shade uncast, a light unshed, or the grey air aswirl with vain entelechies?" (p. 220).

There follows a chain of reflections typical of Watt, in which he tries to decide on a course of action. This ends with Watt submitting to his fate; he grows tired, stoops, and remains motionless for a time. While he is in this "lamentable" position, and while his mind is distracted for a time from his worries, he begins to feel a bit more cheerful.

After this odd description, Watt finds himself underway, that is, in the avenue between the house and the road, with no apparent transition. He has left Micks without saying any words of farewell, thus showing a deficiency in basic courtesy: "The few simple words at parting, that mean so much to him who stays, to him who goes . . ." (p. 222).

The night is unusually bright; the stars shine on Watt and on the beauties of the garden. To Watt's horror, however, it is

> a light so strong, so pure, so steady and so white, that his progress, though painful, and uncertain, was less painful, less uncertain, than he had apprehended, when setting out. (P. 223)

Watt arrives at the train station to find it shut, and he remains standing at the wicket, admiring the tracks. Finally, he climbs over the wicket, picks up his bags again on the other side, and passes around the corner of a wall to arrive on the platform, where he sees a light burning in the signal box. The signalman, Mr. Case, is waiting for the express to pass so that he can set his signals. Watt asks Mr. Case for the time and learns, "It was as he feared, earlier than he hoped" (p. 228).

Watt asks to be let into the waiting room, but this is a delicate question, and it leads to a lengthy "series" which terminates with Mr. Case wondering whether he has the right to open up the room and trying to decide who has the authority over the keys for the individual rooms of the station. "Mr Case considered all this, . . . weighing the for, and weighing the against, without passion" (p. 230). He finally decides to lock Watt into the waiting room overnight and, without giving the reasons for his decision, he says to Watt:

> In the morning . . . you will be let out, and free to come and go, as you please. Watt replied that that would indeed be something to look forward to, and a comfort to him during the night. (P. 231)

Watt lies down on a bench in the waiting room, with his hat over his face:

> Thus the moon was in a measure kept off, and the lesser beauties of this glorious night. The problem of vision, as far as Watt was concerned, admitted of only one solution: the eye open in the dark. The results given by the closed eye were, in Watt's opinion, most unsatisfactory. (P. 232)

Part of the waiting room is faintly lit. Watt finds that, as far as he can see, there is no furniture or any other object in it.

> This did not strike him as strange. Nor did it strike him as usual. For his impression was, such as it was, *as he drooped sigmoidal in its midst*, that this was a *waiting-room*. (P. 233; *italics added*)

All of Watt's thoughts in the waiting room will be discussed again in the following sections of this study.

Then a merry whistling can be heard in the distance. Mr. Nolan, the porter, is approaching. He kicks open the door to the waiting room. Watt, who is standing within range of the door (double doors, the two halves of which move in semicircles), is struck. "Now I am at liberty, said Watt, I am free to come and go, as I please" (p. 238). He peers up at the "four armpits" where the friezes meet as Mr. Nolan greets the stationmaster, Mr. Gorman, at the threshold. That Watt now sees the whiteness of the waiting room ceiling with "extreme distinctness" shows that he has been knocked to the floor by the blow from the door.

Thus Watt has completed another period of residence and another journey, both of which have obviously been conveyed to the reader from Watt's own perspective; he now appears again in a frame situation. Now, however, as at the beginning of *Watt*, it is from the bystanders' point of view that the reader is informed. Watt is no longer the narrator, nor is he any longer the source that whispers everything that is told to Sam. On the contrary, he is now the object of an omniscient narrator.

It has also become obvious that Watt has in a sense become a "fallen man." Watt loses consciousness at the threshold of the waiting room and is out of reach of immediate help. At this point we read "Hiatus in MS." Mr. Gorman looks at his watch: "It was as he feared, later than he hoped" (p. 239). This is a variation of the statement on page 228, "It was as he feared, earlier than he hoped." The one statement occurs just before Watt is let into the waiting room, the second at the point when he is about to leave it and is lying stunned on the floor. Mr. Gorman orders Mr. Nolan, the porter:

> Run fetch a bucket of water, he said, perhaps who knows if we souse him thoroughly he will get up of his own free will. (P. 239)

Mr. Nolan suggests, "Perhaps the hose —," but he fetches the bucket, filled with slimy water, from the pump. While all this is going on, Watt is listening in his head to fragments of poetry by Hölderlin:

.... *von Klippe zu Klippe geworfen*
Endlos ins .... *hinab.*[77]

Mr. Gorman helps Mr. Nolan to dump the bucket of water, heavy with slime, onto the prostrate man. Accidentally the bucket falls on Watt, injuring him:

> Blood now perfused the slime. Mr Gorman and Mr Nolan were not alarmed. It was unlikely that a vital organ was touched. (P. 241)

Mr. Nolan avers, "I declare to God she sprang out of me hands, like as if she was alive" (p. 241). The scene is heartless and brutal. The working-class slang (*she* sprang out of *me* hands, like as if *she* was alive) also suggests a certain vulgarity.

Other characters now appear—other travelers who participate in observing the calamity to which Watt has fallen victim. The names of these bystanders also strike a vulgar tone: Arsy Cox, Herring-gut Waller, Cack-faced Miller. Warm handshakes are exchanged and everyone wishes everyone

77. Apparently drawn from memory, Beckett's quotation in German from Hölderlin's poem (p. 239) is inaccurate. Where Beckett has ". . . von Klippe zu Klippe geworfen / Endlos ins . . . hinab," the actual passage in "Hyperions Schicksalslied" reads, "Wie Wasser von Klippe zu Klippe geworfen, Jahr lang ins Ungewisse hinab." The preceding lines are: "Es schwinden, es fallen Die leidenden Menschen Blindlings von einer Stunde zur andern . . ." (The whole passage reads in English: "Suffering mankind grows weaker, falls blindly from one hour to the next, . . . like water thrown from cliff to cliff, year after year down into uncertainty.") It is impossible not to draw parallels between the poem and the situation described in *Watt*, and to find that "Hyperion's Song of Destiny" is an apt characterization of the mood of the novel.

else a good morning. Mr. Case is uncertain whether the man on the floor is the same person he had seen the night before, when Watt arrived from his journey to the station. It seems to Mr. Case that Watt is wearing the same clothes and the same hat and has the same bags, but he does not recognize Watt's face, even though he scrapes off some of the slime.

As everyone is gathered around Watt, a "messenger" arrives, an out-of-breath boy who reports that Mr. Cole has sent him. Because Lady McCann does not know who Mr. Cole is, Mr. Case explains, "of the level-crossing, my lady." No more is said of his identity. Mr. Cole wants to know why Mr. Case's signals are against Mr. Cole's five fifty-seven from the southeast and the six six from the northwest. (Mr. Cole apparently has some control over the trains.) Lady McCann sends the boy back to Mr. Cole with a message:

> Tell him that — has been the scene of terrible events, but that now all is well. Repeat now after me. The scene . . . . . . of terrible . . . . . . terrible . . . . . . events . . . . . . but that now . . . . . . all is well . . . . . . (P. 243)

When Watt finally does stand up, Mr. Gorman asks, "Who the devil are you . . . and what the hell do you want?" (p. 243). Watt finds his hat and puts it on, finds his bags and picks them up.

Watt walks out to the booking office where he orders his ticket, accompanied all the while by the derisive comments of the bystanders. He requests a ticket "to the end of the line." A few minutes later the six four pulls in.

> The sun was now well above the visible horizon. Mr Gorman, Mr Case, and Mr Nolan turned their faces towards it, as men will, in the early morning, without heeding. (P. 245)

The story thus ends without any definite information as to where Watt has gone. It can be assumed that he is on his way to the end of the line. The story concludes with the three railway employees taking their leave of each other, each proceeding in a separate direction. Mr. Case delays a bit, however, turns around, and asks:

> And our friend? . . .
> Friend? . . .
> Is it the long wet dream with the hat and bags?
> (P. 246)

The three look out

> at nothing in particular, though the sky falling to the hills, and the hills falling to the plain, made as pretty a picture, in the early morning light, as a man could hope to meet with, in a day's march. (P. 246)

The section entitled "Addenda" follows. This includes material apparently not intended as a possible continuation of the narrative, but rather material which was simply not suitable for incorporation into the novel (that is, notes or sketches). Beckett obviously considered them important and characteristic enough to publish them, even if only as an appendix.

Summary of the Sequence of Events

Watt makes his first appearance in the evening as he gets off a tram. This and his subsequent motionlessness are observed by a small group of secondary characters. Watt then proceeds to the train station where he collides with a porter who is moving milk cans about. Watt begins his journey from that point by train. Because the train barely pauses at his destination, Watt must jump off quickly. He then proceeds along the road, wearing his hat and carrying his bags in his hands. After a certain distance he lies down at the edge of a ditch, only to roll down into the ditch (where he hears a choir singing) shortly thereafter. He is then able to continue his journey to Mr. Knott's house "with less effort than he had feared." Although the doors of Mr. Knott's house are closed at first, Watt manages to cross the threshold, without knowing exactly how, and sits down in the kitchen. There Arsene, the departing servant, tells him a long story, referred to as a "short statement." Then Watt begins his work in Mr. Knott's house, first on the ground floor, then on the second floor. He serves Mr. Knott his food, which he prepares according to a complicated set of instructions, and disposes of the leftovers, which must always be set out for a hungry dog so that they are completely devoured. He encounters Mr. Knott rarely at first, then more frequently, especially after Erskine, the servant on the second floor when Watt arrives, departs and Watt has to take his place.

After a long excursion into the gardens in which the pavilions are located (Watt has moved into another one, leaving Sam behind) and an episode of reversed events which leads to a partial reunion of Watt and Sam (they walk about between the separate gardens together, one backward, the other forward), Watt returns to Mr. Knott's house. Arthur, Watt's successor on the ground floor, relates a long story. Mr. Knott, who undergoes a constant series of transformations in his physical appearance, is described as well as possible. In spite of the continuous change in Mr. Knott's house and garden, spiritual tranquility (ataraxy) prevails. Watt separates again from Sam and disappears into his pavilion.

Mr. Micks arrives, the successor to Arthur on the ground floor. This is when Watt must leave Mr. Knott's service. Watt stands in the kitchen to bid farewell, where once Arsene had stood when Watt arrived. Watt is again wearing his hat and holding his bags (which are now called grousebags and which appear to be smaller than before).

Watt departs with great composure but says no words of farewell. In the avenue between the house and the road he stops and notices the beauty of the stars and the garden. Without transition he bursts into tears on the road. He finally arrives at the train station where he must spend the night locked in the waiting room. In the morning he is knocked to the floor stunned when the double doors to the waiting room are flung open. Two railway employees douse him with a bucket of cold, slimy water and injure him accidentally as the bucket slips from their hands. Watt revives; he picks up his hat and bags again and buys a ticket to the end of the line. It is now morning and the six four arrives, which Watt apparently boards. The bystanders continue to comment on his appearance and disappearance, just as his arrival on the tram before his other train journey was witnessed by another group of secondary characters. A new summer day begins.

The House in Roussillon, Vaucluse, in which Beckett lived when writing Watt

View of Rousillon

View of Roussillon

Beckett in Berlin, 1967

Samuel Beckett (left) and Gottfried Büttner (right), Berlin 1967

The Composition and Formal Aspects of Watt

It's the shape that matters.
  Samuel Beckett[78]

III

---

78. See Pilling, *Samuel Beckett*, p. 1. According to a personal communication from Pilling, this remark by Beckett appears in an article in *L'Express*, February 8, 1957, p. 26.

Preliminary Remarks and Stylistic Examples

This study presents an analysis of the text of Samuel Beckett's *Watt* with regard to its value as a source of knowledge—its inner content. No preconceived ideas are read into the text. In this chapter the composition of the novel as a whole and its formal features will be discussed. A general interpretation of the content will then be attempted in chapter 4.

Beckett does not make it easy for the reader to integrate large portions of this novel into a logical whole. The consideration of *Watt*'s formal features and overall composition serves here merely to discover clues to its gnosiologically relevant content. Chapter 3 therefore does not involve a formal study of surface structure; rather, it lays the groundwork for the interpretation developed in the following chapter. It should be kept in mind at all times that this act of interpreting is not to be confused with "explaining."

I agree completely with Wolfgang Iser's view that the conventional critical approach is a phenomenon of the nineteenth century. In his opinion, critical standards formed on the basis of classical ideals omit a crucial dimension from the reader's experience of a text.[79] Particularly in the case of contemporary literature, the reader is not called upon to indulge in sympathetic contemplation, but rather to participate actively in the creation of meaning. This meaning embraces the reader, because only in him does meaning acquire existential reality.[80]

The text of *Watt* is not *explained* in this study as part of a certain "frame of reference," but is rather presented in terms of its value to the reader. All the same, the position is defended here that, by virtue of its symbolic character, the text must also be valid with respect to homo sapiens as the ideal.

Studies of the linguistic style of *Watt* have been listed in

---

79. *The Act of Reading*, pp. 5ff., 152.
80. Ibid., p. 151. Iser refers here to Ricoeur, who in turn picks up the ideas of Frege and Husserl.

the section on secondary literature in chapter 1. I refer in particular to the comprehensive studies by Horst and Rolf Breuer, Ursula Dreysse, John Fletcher, James Knowlson, and John Pilling. Manfred Smuda's study, *Becketts Prosa als Metasprache,*[81] Wolfgang Iser's "The Pattern of Negativity in Beckett's Prose,"[82] and the other works by Iser already mentioned also belong here. Marianne Kesting has investigated esthetic aspects of Beckett's work in "Das Romanwerk Samuel Becketts."[83] Jean-Jacques Mayoux has also analyzed Beckett's style. In his view, Beckett comes extremely close to the "visionary art of projection."[84]

The unique character of Beckett's style is not the concern here, however. Beckett's vocabulary, syntax, and speech rhythms are not at issue, and the formal nature of *Watt* is of interest only with regard to the structure of the whole. Therefore, in addition to the "macrostructure" of the composition of the four parts of the novel, I deal only with a few stylistic examples which I view as associated "microstructures." All other aspects of this topic must be omitted.

Mayoux has written about Beckett: "Even if Beckett does appear to be obscure at first glance, it is found on closer inspection that the meaning of his work is never on the surface and must always be translated first into everyday language."[85] This confirms the relevance of a study, such as that presented here, on the hidden, gnosiological content of *Watt*.

Watt is situated, not only chronologically but also stylistically, between the early fiction, such as *More Pricks Than Kicks* and *Murphy,* and the later works in French. Beckett has already developed here a distance from language characteristic of his later writing. To write "without style" is one of the reasons Beckett has given for adopting French. Iser views

81. Munich, 1970.

82. *The Georgia Review* 29 (1975): 706–19.

83. In her *Vermessung des Labyrinths: Studien zur modernen Ästhetik* (Frankfurt am Main, 1965).

84. *Über Beckett* (Frankfurt am Main, 1966), p. 11.

85. Ibid., p. 9.

Beckett's language as pure denotation; that is, an effort is made to eliminate implications and suppress connotations. In linguistics such texts are termed nonreferential fiction. The elements of repeated negation and the retraction of what has been said in order to annul meaning are already present in *Watt*, although not in the highly developed form found in the trilogy. For the rest, we must agree with Rolf Breuer that "even less than in the earlier works does a plot summary of *Watt* convey anything of the impression created by actually reading the novel. This impression is determined largely by the style and the rhetorical devices."[86]

Watt begins in the manner of an entirely conventional novel with an apparently traditional, omniscient narrator. This conformity with convention lasts until the first footnote, which has already been mentioned. In terms of theme, *Watt* is similar to *Murphy*. An example of this is the scene in which Mr. Hackett tries to enlist the services of a policeman in putting a stop to the immoral behavior of the lovers sitting on "his" seat:

> Mr Hackett decided, after some moments, that if they were waiting for a tram they had been doing so for some time. For the lady held the gentleman by the ears, and the gentleman's hand was on the lady's thigh, and the lady's tongue was in the gentleman's mouth. Tired of waiting for the tram, said Mr Hackett, they strike up an acquaintance. The lady now removing her tongue from the gentleman's mouth, he put his into hers. Fair do, said Mr Hackett. Taking a pace forward, to satisfy himself that the gentleman's other hand was not going to waste, Mr Hackett was shocked to find it limply dangling over the back of the seat, with between its fingers the spent three quarters of a cigarette.
>
> I see no indecency, said the policeman.
>
> We arrive too late, said Mr Hackett. What a shame.

86. *Die Kunst der Paradoxie*, p. 63.

Do you take me for a fool? said the policeman.

Mr Hackett recoiled a step, forced back his head until he thought his throatskin would burst, and saw at last, afar, bent angrily upon him, the red violent face. (Pp. 8–9)

This passage illustrates the rapid sequence of statements typical of Beckett's style. But, in addition to the precision of expression associated with this style, it also reveals a dramatic element that replaces description with action. We do not read, "Mr. Hackett was overly short of stature, and the policeman was a big, husky fellow." On the contrary, we read how Mr. Hackett must bend his head back—almost tearing his throatskin—until he can finally see, far away, the red, violent face of the policeman who is angrily bending over him. The situation is not explained; instead, the figures are placed in the scene, where they reveal their individualizing characteristics through their behavior. This is the language of a dramatist.

As the narrative proceeds, it is not only the dramatic structure that evolves. As Watt leaves the realms of existence that are accessible to external description, the narrative point of view changes and the interior of the soul is entered. The normal laws of the environment are negated and our everyday set of terms and definitions loses its validity. Critics such as John Chalker[87] are of the opinion that the entire narrative structure "collapses," which not only makes it odd and enervating to read *Watt*, but also gives the impression that "the form itself becomes a satiric representation of a failure."[88]

I do not see here a "failure syndrome." On the contrary, Beckett's language is precise even where words (very nearly) fail, because as the rational, three-dimensional world is abandoned as an object of conscious awareness, language is free to be transformed even more thoroughly into a metaphorical

87. "The Satiric Shape of *Watt*," in *Beckett the Shape Changer*, ed. Katherine Worth (London, 1975), pp. 21–37.

88. Ibid., p. 29.

means of expression. As foreshadowed in the story of the piano tuner Gall and his son (p. 70), loss of identity or even of being is characteristic of a departure from ordinary planes of consciousness. The same problem is embodied in the passages about the pot, which could just as well be a vase or a box. The correlation between things or words and certain meanings is lost. A "transvaluation of all values" must be carried out in view of the dissociation of universally known facts from their conventional meanings. Language assumes here a purely imagistic function, which must be understood anew in its own terms.

Examples of this style, which can be called nonreferential, are found primarily in part III, where the gardens in which Watt and Sam come and go are described. The two are forced to communicate with each other through barbed wire fences. It is difficult to find adequate words to describe these mental and spiritual barriers, and the attempt to do so continually breaks down and starts over again from the beginning. First the two friends are separated by a small brook, then by ditches, and finally by a double line of barbed wire fences. A great deal of mental agility is required to find access to one region from the other. Fat people (spiritually lazy ones) have particular difficulty. Here spiritual dimensions are concealed behind physical relationships.

The precision of Beckett's language is exemplified by the following paragraph, given first in French from the edition prepared by Agnes and Ludovic Janvier with Beckett's substantial help.

> A travers cette clôture, là où elle n'était pas aveuglée par des ronces et des orties géantes, se voyaient distinctement de toutes parts des parcs semblables, semblablement enclos, chacun avec son pavillon. Tantôt divergeant, tantôt convergeant, ces clôtures dessinaient des lacis d'une irrégularité frappante. Nulle clôture n'était mitoyenne, ne fût-ce qu'en partie. Mais leur proximité était telle, à certains endroits, qu'un homme large

d'épaules ou de bassin, enfilant cette passe étroite, le ferait avec plus de facilité, et avec moins de danger pour sa veste, et peut-être pour son pantalon, de biais que de front. En revanche, pour un homme gros de fesses ou de ventre, l'attaque directe s'imposerait, sous peine de se voir perforer l'estomac, ou le cul, peut-être les deux d'une ou de plusieurs barbes rouillées.[89]

In the original, this passage reads:

Through this fence, where it was not overgrown by briars and giant nettles, similar gardens, similarly enclosed, each with its pavilion, were on all sides distinctly to be seen. Now converging, now diverging, these fences presented a striking irregularity of contour. No fence was party, nor any part of any fence. But their adjacence was such, at certain places, that a broad-shouldered or broad-basined man, threading these narrow straits, would have done so with greater ease, and with less jeopardy to his coat, and perhaps to his trousers, sideways than frontways. For a big-bottomed man, on the contrary, or a big-bellied man, frontal motion would be an absolute necessity, if he did not wish his stomach to be perforated, or his arse, or perhaps both, by a rusty barb, or by rusty barbs. (Pp. 156–57)

The connotation-free language that Beckett uses is, as Iser also points out,[90] a purely objective language: "But Beckett writes novels, and as fiction these do not denote any given, empirical world; they should therefore conform to the literary conventions of using the denotative function of language to build up connotations which may then be grasped as units of meaning. Instead, Beckett takes language literally."[91]

89. *Watt* (Paris: Edition de Minuit, 1968), p. 186.
90. *The Act of Reading*, p. 222.
91. Ibid., p. 223.

It is assumed here that Beckett does in fact produce "fiction," which in a purely external sense is of course correct. But why does he do this with the language of "nonfiction"? He uses an objective language because he describes something that for him has the character of reality—"objects" belonging to the next-higher order of being which he experiences just as other people experience tables and chairs. All the same, he must develop his own (poetic) language for this purpose. If he were to allow connotations as well, they would only distract attention from this process (see chapter 4, pp. 108ff. and 154ff.).

Beckett's language is precise, concise, and "realistic," except that it is spoken on a metaphorical level of narration. It might be useful to recall that the concept of "realism" does not originate with the literary period thus designated, but rather designates a philosophical current that posits the content of reality of abstract ideas (in contrast to nominalism). Realism assumes an external world independent of the knower, which includes so-called transcendental realism. Beckett is in this sense an "ideal realist" who denotes *reality.*

The stylistic element of inversion so characteristic of part III of *Watt* is discussed in detail in chapter 3, pp. 94ff. In part III as well, extreme discipline and economy of language are evident. The following words of Rolf Breuer particularly apply to this part of *Watt:* "The novel *Watt* begins the series of works that alienate the unprepared reader to the extreme." Beckett has written a text "which, in its bizarre mixture of *compassion* and madness, has the effect of being inexplicably uncontemporary."[92] Almost every sentence will appear absurd to the "unprepared reader."

The special poetry of Beckett's prose is experienced by the reader whenever Beckett returns to the normal world, that is, whenever he leads Watt back to a point of rest, for example at the end of a chapter and thus at the end of a unit of action.

---

92. Breuer, *Die Kunst der Paradoxie,* p. 62.

The passage at the end of the first part, for example, in which the hope of a new day is expressed, corresponds to a similar passage at the end of the fourth part, in which a new summer day begins and in which, as so often happens, a goat appears. These two passages read as follows:

> For if it was really day again already, in some low distant quarter of the sky, it was not yet day again already in the kitchen. But that would come, Watt knew that would come, with patience it would come, little by little, whether he liked it or not, over the yard wall, and through the window, first the grey, then the brighter colours one by one, until getting on to nine a.m. all the gold and white and blue would fill the kitchen, all the unsoiled light of the new day, of the new day at last, the day without precedent at last. (P. 64)

> The road lay still, at this hour, leaden, deserted, between its hedges, and its ditches. From one of these latter a goat emerged, dragging its pale and chain. The goat hesitated, in the middle of the road, then turned away. The clatter came fainter and fainter, down the still air, and came still faintly when the pale had disappeared, beyond the rise. The trembling sea could not but be admired. The leaves quivered, or gave the impression of doing so, and the grasses also, beneath the drops, or beads, of gaily expiring dew. (P. 245)

Although the lyric-romantic sound of these passages is unmistakable, Beckett's overall style is anything but "romantic." There are passages that suggest this element, however, especially the rare occasions, as here, when Beckett evokes the moods of nature. Most of these evocations are melancholy, but I doubt that Lawrence E. Harvey is correct when he writes, "If Beckett has a romantic side, it surely appears most clearly in the melancholy that accompanies the numerous manifestations of nothingness."[93] I believe it is precisely when nothingness becomes manifest that Beckett prefers "sober denotation," to borrow Iser's apt phrase. That is, in these cases Beckett tends to use purely objective language. The poetry appears only after nothingness has been transcended. In this sense, even denotations—provided the reader knows how to receive them—can contribute to the poetry of the work as a whole. It is this stylistic element in particular that both constitutes the realistic character of Beckett's prose and gives it a delicate, understated poetic finish.

The Interrelationships Among the Four Parts *of* Watt

The following passage appears at the very beginning of part IV:

> As Watt told the beginning of his story, not first, but second, so not fourth, but third, now he told its end. Two, one, four, three, that was the order in which Watt told his story. (P. 215)

Initially it might seem that these words describe the sequence in which the author actually wrote the novel. This account of the divisions of the book is certainly perplexing in any case. Fundamentally, however, this is not an attempt to confuse the reader, as Beckett occasionally loves to do, nor is it merely a clever twisting of the chronology of the four parts of the novel. On the contrary, the rearrangement of the four parts is both thought provoking and informative.

The most important part of Watt's story takes place in parts II and III in Mr. Knott's house. We can understand, therefore, when it is stated that Watt began his story "sec-

---

93. "Samuel Beckett—initiation du poète" in *Samuel Beckett—Configuration critique*, ed. Melvin J. Friedman (Paris, 1964), p. 153.

ond." It is also probable that the third part belongs at the end, since Watt's experiences described there are, in a sense, the goal of the entire undertaking.

Part I describes only Watt's *appearance* and his journey to Mr. Knott's house and gives a preview of parts II and III in Arsene's "statement," just before Arsene's departure from the house. In just the same way, Watt is in the act of *leaving* Mr. Knott's house when part IV begins; I and IV thus have an inner relationship and, so to speak, play on the same plane of experience. Parts I and IV now follow one another as the result of the new sequence (II, I, IV, III).

Parts II and III still follow chronologically, but they are now shifted to the beginning and the end. They correspond to each other as mirror images; they, too, embody related dimensions and are qualitatively the same, but they follow in sequence only when we imagine the parts of the novel as a closed circle.

Seen in this new way, the four parts actually do provide a meaningful arrangement in the order under discussion here—that is, two, one, four, three. Part IV follows part I; parts II and III form the beginning and end and function like mirror images. If we assume this "absurd" order as *given*, then the first sentence reads normally again and actually provides the real order: Watt began his story second, that is, with part I. He tells the end third, that is, in part IV. Externally this is correct; internally, however, the "shuffled" sequence is also completely correct because it corresponds to the qualitatively different narrative or experiential planes.[94]

94. The breakup of the temporal sequence is evident again through this "new arrangement" at the beginning of part IV of *Watt*. A *qualitative* order replaces the linear sequence of events. Prior to Beckett, the break with linear time was justified subjectively as an expression of "stream of consciousness." Examples of similar subjective associations which are in fact independent of linear time structure are to be found since Sterne in Marcel Proust, James Joyce, Virginia Woolf, Aldous Huxley, and Henry James. This also suggests a necessary evolution which transcends the subjective (see chapter 4, pp. 163–164.).

Parts II and III

We can assume that what Watt reports from Mr. Knott's house and garden is qualitatively different from what is said about Watt when he is located elsewhere. If we consider the sequence of events on the basis of the revised structural relationships, many irregularities and inversions suddenly become clear. For this reason, I begin with part II (the "real" beginning) and then turn to the "real" ending, part III.

If we accept the initial hypothesis that Mr. Knott's house and garden are to be found elsewhere—that is, in another world, another realm of existence—it is no wonder that in the first section we read of Watt's hope of one day being face to face with Mr. Knott, an experience that Arsene, who has just left the house, has probably enjoyed, and one that Erskine, who has now moved upstairs, is probably now enjoying. Mr. Knott is called master (*maître* in French), as I pointed out earlier in the summary.

Watt's expectant attitude toward meeting the unknown Mr. Knott is reminiscent of *Waiting for Godot*. The only difference is that, as matters proceed, this "Godot"—that is, Mr. Knott—becomes "visible," at least in anthropomorphic terms, whereas the actual Godot (of the play) remains invisible and only sends his messenger.

Furthermore, it has already been pointed out that Mr. Knott's world is characterized by a rigid hierarchy: when the time comes for the upstairs servant to leave, the ground-floor servant moves up to replace him, at which point a new man arrives to fill the vacancy downstairs. Thus there is a sequence of countless generations of servants. The names of a few of these predecessors are mentioned (Vincent, Walter, Arsene, Erskine, whom Watt follows, later to be followed himself by Arthur and finally by Micks). In addition, the master keeps his distance and allows himself to be served. Everything revolves around him, even though he remains out of sight for the most part. Visitors from the outside are rare.

What is the nature of this "other world" of Mr. Knott's

house? Our first clue is the story of the Galls, father and son, who come to tune the broken piano. What is of interest here is explained after this remarkable visit is over; it throws a characteristic light on the changed mode of existence and on the modes of thought and experience associated with it.

The first striking aspect of the Galls' visit is that, in contrast to our expectation, it is not the blind piano tuner, the father, but rather the son that does the work. It seems illogical, therefore, that the old man has come along at all. This suggests that the entire concept of "meaning" has changed, in that events now signify something both while they are happening and as they appear in retrospect. Furthermore, the events are only occasions, not ends in themselves; that is, they are referential in character: they point to something else, to something other than what they appear to be on the surface. Style and all its devices are calculated to show this.

This visit by the Galls, which is called the "principal incident," thus resembles all the other "remarkable incidents" that occur during Watt's stay in Mr. Knott's house:

> It resembled them in the sense that it was not ended, when it was past, but continued to unfold, in Watt's head, . . . according to the irrevocable caprice of its taking place. (P. 72)

The key sentence that defines this ability of events to contain their meaning in their reference to something else, at least as far as Watt is concerned, is:

> This fragility of the outer meaning had a bad effect on Watt, for it caused him to seek for another, for some meaning of what had passed, in the image of how it had passed. (P. 73)

This recalls Goethe's dictum, "Das Was bedenke, mehr bedenke Wie," but here we are speaking in an epistemological sense, not a psychological one.

The formal aspects of the narrative do justice to this orientation. Whatever "incidents" Watt encounters, everything that happens in Mr. Knott's house and garden has this referential or imagistic character. Nothing simply occurs; nothing is an end in itself. The "how" of the occurrence is the occasion for reflection, evocation of memories, and so on. This is exemplified by the Galls' remarkable visit:

> The incident of the Galls, on the contrary, ceased so rapidly to have even the paltry significance of two men, come to tune a piano, and tuning it, and exchanging a few words, as men will do, and going, that this seemed rather to belong to some story heard long before. (P. 74)

Watt, therefore, frequently does not know *what* has happened, but he needs to know that a certain incident *did* occur and to know why it occurred at that particular time. He needs to be able to say, "Yes, I remember, this is what happened then" (p. 74). This need remains with Watt during the greater part of his stay in Mr. Knott's house.

Watt also suspected (correctly) that such incidents are unknown outside Mr. Knott's house and garden, but he would rather not accept them for the "simple games which time plays with space."

> Add to this the notorious difficulty of recapturing, at will, modes of feeling peculiar to a certain time, and to a certain place, and perhaps also to a certain state of the health, when the time is past, and the place left, and the body struggling with quite a new situation . . . Add to this the scant aptitude to give of him to whom they were committed. And some idea will perhaps be obtained of the difficulties experienced in formulating, not only such matters as those here in question, but *the entire body of Watt's experience,* from the moment of his entering Mr Knott's establishment to the moment of his leaving it. (P. 75; *emphasis added*)

In particular, Watt's frequent complaints alert the reader to the new state of his consciousness. He not only has problems perceiving what happens, but also has difficulty expressing himself understandably. He speaks in a low, rapid voice and his syntax is eccentric. The source of these difficulties is the knowledge that is derived from nothingness.

The reader must learn to read and understand these incidents for what they are: occasions for reflection, sketches which have reality in their *imagistic* character and which acquire substance only when the reader provides it by giving them meaning. We can do this only after we have attuned ourselves to the incidents, enter into their world, and thus understand them. For Watt, the result of all this is a "loss of being," but this is a loss to which he gradually—and painfully—becomes accustomed. Watt seeks desperately for a confirmation of self as an antidote to alienation. By paying close attention to what goes on around him, he attempts to acquire new powers of perception which will enable him to find his bearings in this new world.

These efforts are expressed in the so-called series, which of course also demonstrate the futility of using logic to achieve a sense of orientation. Rolf Breuer distinguishes four types of such mathematical "games" in Beckett: (1) the purely quantitative type (rhetorically we would speak here of an enumeration, catalog, or list); (2) the sequential type; (3) the combinatorial type; and (4) the permutational type. There are also mixed forms of these style-forming serial or combinatorial passages.[95]

These pseudological excesses should not be confused with florid aberrations, for this would underestimate their function. Nor are they poetic effusions, which fill page after page simply to display formal brilliance. Rather, they are the expression of an uncompromising effort to obtain clarity and to escape the constraints of external, superficial meaning.

---

95. *Die Kunst der Paradoxie,* p. 65. (See also the studies by François Martel and John J. Mood.)

As tedious mathematical problems, the "series" also have an educating effect, insofar as they exercise the mind. The problems they present are irrelevant in light of their development of our mental powers. Here again, meaning is primarily in the "how," not in the "what."

These formal exercises fill many pages of *Watt* and constitute the bulk of part II. After the pot, it is the food; after the food, it is the disposal of the leftovers by the dogs; then it is the Lynch family with its plethora of absurd relationships and its job of providing dogs to eat the leftovers.[96]

When Erskine's behavior is described—it is characterized by a constant rushing up and down stairs—the words also become hurried. In the series on the bell in Erskine's room, it becomes obvious that whoever lives in the upper regions of the house is in fact totally "out of his mind." To obtain greater clarity, Watt decides to break into Erskine's room, even though this will eventually be his own room after Erskine has left Mr. Knott's employ. The following passage describes Watt's response to the difficulty of understanding what he experiences:

> Watt did not care to enquire in so many words into the meaning of all this, for he said, All this will be revealed to Watt, in due time. (P. 119)

One day, at the proper moment, the revelation will come and Watt will learn what he was unable to discover by his own efforts. Nevertheless, Watt's curiosity gets the better of him. He insists on getting to the bottom of the mysterious relationship between Erskine and Mr. Knott, and for this reason he breaks into Erskine's room. He finds nothing but a

---

96. The name "Lynch" for this family striving to survive for a thousand years is certainly not accidental. Rolf Breuer sees in it an ironic connection with the Nazi regime and its paladins (see *Die Kunst der Paradoxie*, p. 62 n.).

broken bell and a picture hanging on the wall, the meaning of which we will discuss later. Pictures must "explain" what is meant when words fail.

The acausality of events is made evident in another series which deals with Mr. Knott's servants (Tom, Dick, Harry, etc.). Not one of them comes, goes, or stays *because of* any of the others, but rather only because Tom is Tom, Dick Dick, and Harry Harry. And even though Mr. Knott is referred to here as a harbor and a haven, a linguistic chaos of words (although carefully contrived) surrounds him until all plain meaning becomes confused and disappears, and even the mathematical word game of a "frog's chorus" represents a certain reassuring "clarity" to Watt.

After Watt manages to open this particular "tin" with his "blowlamp," he finds that it is empty after all. He has opened a sort of Pandora's box from which nothing but meaningless words escape. Even words have lost their identity.

Two characters who incite speculation appear next: the fishwoman and the gardener. What is their relationship to Watt and what roles do they play? "The fishwoman pleased Watt greatly" (p. 138). Every Thursday she comes to Watt, and they express their love by alternately sitting on each other's lap. Her name is Mrs. Gorman. "Mrs Gorman had had several admirers, both before and after Mr Gorman, and even during Mr Gorman" (p. 139).

The love relationship between Watt and Mrs. Gorman, the fishwoman, is highly grotesque and should be read as a parody of the sexual behavior of man and woman. The scene reenacts the futile labors of love intended to generate new life. The otherwise inexplicable name "fishwoman," which suggests that she is slimy, slippery, and cold, seems to underscore this. The encounter occurring every Thursday leads to nothing, "For Watt had not the strength, and Mrs Gorman had not the time, indispensable to even the most perfunctory coalescence" (p. 141).

Mr. Graves comes to the back door four times a day. In

the morning he fetches the key to the shed, at noon he gets a pot of tea, in the afternoon a bottle of stout, and in the evening he returns the key. He is one of the estate personnel, the gardener. He wears a hard hat, which he devotedly removes even in the open air when speaking with his betters. He appears not only at this stage of the novel but also at various other times throughout it. He does not get along well with his wife and hopes for Watt's advice. He knows all there is to know about Mr. Knott and all his servants, and is able to recount many things about them, but nothing of interest. His father, and his father's father, and so forth, had all worked for Mr. Knott. His family, he says, made the garden what it is. It is difficult to avoid the impression that the gardener is a personification of death. The name "Graves" supports this assumption.

Watt ascends the rungs of this hierarchically ordered world, beginning his service on the ground floor. In due course the gardener acknowledges Watt's new social status: "This was the first time that Watt had been assimilated to the class of young gentlemen" (p. 143). Just before the end of part II it is mentioned that Watt occasionally "catches a glimpse" of Mr. Knott in the vestibule or garden. Once he encounters Mr. Knott sleeping. He does not know whether he should be happy or sad that he sees his master so rarely.

A mood of the undecided, of the undecidable, pervades the entire second part. At the end, the question of whether Watt has learned anything at all on the ground floor remains unanswered. When Arthur arrives and Erskine comes down the stairs, Watt knows that it is time for him to ascend to the second floor.

As for the structure of part III of *Watt* and its special features, it has already been noted that it does not appear to connect smoothly with part II. There is a break here. If we take what has been said up to now about the superficiality of *literal meaning* seriously, that is, that words can only approximate what is really meant, we can understand where Watt has now arrived.

Watt has in fact ascended to the second floor of Mr. Knott's house, even though we read that he has moved to "another pavilion." What does a move to another house, a new residence, mean? Certainly it means a separation from the past or even a totally new frame of reference. We quickly realize that Watt is no longer just Watt, but that he now has a partner, Sam, who functions as Watt's alter ego. Sam continues to obtain information from Watt, but he represents a consciousness which has separated or split itself off from him. Although this cleavage suggests schizophrenia, the split is not pathological; it is controlled and can be overcome or reversed at any time, as in fact occurs. Here no one is a victim, but there is no doubt that this state of consciousness resembles that of a deranged person. This has already been mentioned in the earlier summary. Beckett's choice of imagery appropriately expresses the two spheres of consciousness— Watt and Sam: each has his own little fenced-in garden, his separate field of consciousness, and the manner in which each gets about in his garden is characteristically different. The fences between them have holes, but they have not been opened easily (they have been burst open forcibly); there are streams separating them, but also bridges which can be "repaired." The fence is barbed and injures Watt. From all this it can be inferred that the nature of the second floor of Mr. Knott's house is much more complicated than might be initially believed.

Watt's mode of locomotion is highly characteristic of part III. What Beckett achieves by so accurately describing what is happening to Watt must be discussed in detail. Bodily movement is equivalent here to *moving about mentally,* and in this sense speaking backward (to which thinking backward naturally corresponds) is a logical correlative to Watt's strange movements. The abilities to move and think are not so remote from each other after all. Older cultures understood the relationship between bodily movement and mental activity and created artistic forms based on the connections between dance, song, and language. In *Waiting for Godot* Beckett jokingly points this out, for he is obviously well aware of this relationship.[97]

Walking backward is therefore only another image for *talking* backward, and this in turn refers to a reversal of the thinking process. This different type of thinking—the mirror image of logical, straightforward thinking—can be learned. It is in fact acquired in stages by practice on the second floor of Mr. Knott's house.

We are prepared for the change of scene at the beginning of part III by the building of the bridge between Watt and Sam and the subsequent contact between them as they lie on the bridge. Later it is the holes in the fences which permit them to communicate, although with difficulty. Watt becomes entangled in the barbed wire (we are reminded of a crucifixion scene) after creeping backward toward Sam, who, "like a mad creature" (p. 158), watches Watt's laborious approach. At this point in the text the first reversal—here, of word sequence in the sentence—occurs: Watt answers Sam's question with the words, "Not it is, yes," which should of course be read, "Yes, is it not" (p. 159). These few words cause Sam both alarm and pain, an impression which is immediately reinforced by another inverted sentence, "Wonder I, panky-hanky me lend you could, blood away wipe" (pp. 159–60).

The process of inversion thus begins. Everything in this region is different from what it is in the familiar world; logical order is stood on end.[98] Sam, who wonders how all this has come about (". . . where now I stood, trying to understand" [p. 162]), also wonders, in a series on infuriated animals and

---

97. See *Waiting for Godot* (New York, 1954), p. 26. Estragon: "Perhaps he could dance first and think afterwards, if it isn't too much to ask of him." And Pozzo answers: "By all means, nothing simpler. It's the natural order." The linguistic relationship between *agitare* and *cogitare* in Latin might refer to the same connection between movement and thought.

98. A similar situation is described in Ionesco's *Le pieton de l'air*. See Gottfried Büttner, *Absurdes Theater und Bewusstseinswandel* (Berlin, 1968), pp. 132ff.

violent weather, how the two holes were made in the fencing. He sees Watt, who appears again at his call, with his pants on backward, walking backward as well. He pulls Watt over to his side of the fence and the two join in the manner described, Watt marching backward, Sam forward: "As Watt walked, so now he talked, back to front" (p. 164).

Examples of "Watt's style" in this phase follow. Because Watt speaks backward, the text is naturally unintelligible to the normal reader. Only by actually reading backward, which is simple as long as only the sequence of words is reversed, is it possible to discover that important information is provided, which somehow typifies the situation. The first example of this type begins, *"Day of most, night of part, Knott with now"* and ends with *"Hush in, mist in, moved I so"* (p. 164).

If we read this text in reverse, we learn something about Watt's situation. It describes how Watt passes the time under lightless and soundless conditions—that is, his eyes and ears fail him. It is quiet and misty; he hears and sees this and that, but still manages to absorb very little. He is with Mr. Knott part of the night and much of the day. Step by step, the inversions become more "complete." The words are always meaningless to Sam at first, even though he is strolling along eye to eye with Watt.

The next step is for the sequence of the letters to be reversed. The text on page 165 reads when transposed:

> To orb, blur pale, dark bulk. To drum, low puff, low puff. To skin, gross mass, gross mass. To smell, stale smell. To tongue, tart sweat, tart sweat.

The poetic word "orb" is used here for eye, and "drum" (eardrum) obviously stands for the ear. The orthography is also greatly transformed and simplified. The "a" in "sweat" is omitted, and for the tongue we find only "tung," or rather its backwards form, "gnut." This makes reading difficult.

Between the first two samples of reversed speech we read the following sentence:

> Thus I missed I suppose much I suspect of great interest touching I presume the first or initial stage of the second or closing period of Watt's stay in Mr Knott's house. (P. 165)

The second sample, quoted above, is followed by this sentence:

> Thus I missed I suppose much I presume of great interest touching I suspect the second stage of the second or closing period of Watt's stay in Mr Knott's house. (P. 165)

The second or closing period, that is, Watt's time on the second floor of the house, is recorded in part III (during the split into Watt and Sam). This closing period has a "first stage," a "second stage," and so on, and it is described in an increasingly complicated series of inversions. After each additional inversion there is another reference to this stepwise progression.

In the third stage the sentences in the paragraph are reversed: "Of nought. To the source. To the teacher." Rearranged, the paragraph reads:

> Abandoned my little to find him. My little to learn him forgot. My little rejected to have him. To love him my little reviled. This body homeless. This mind ignoring. These emptied hands. This emptied heart. To him I brought. To the temple. To the teacher. To the source. Of nought. (P. 166)

Watt thus gives up his "little" to find Mr. Knott, to learn him, to have him. He abandons his little, his miserable body and unknowing mind, and empties his hands and heart to love him. Watt has brought all this to the temple, to the teacher, to the source of nothingness. Once we reverse the puzzling, turned-around text, we discover an amazing passage describing Watt's situation.

After this passage on the source of nought (i.e., the second floor of the house in part III), which has the effect of a climax, there are additional entanglements; however this passage represents the high point of Watt's experiences with Mr. Knott. From this point, in terms of the pursuit of knowledge, the dynamics of the narrative slowly ebb away, and at the end of the chapter the reader is returned to a situation similar, but not identical, to that at the beginning. As in the other three parts, a wavelike movement can be observed.

A new source of confusion is encountered next in the reversal of both the words in the sentence and the letters in the word: "Deen did taw? Tonk. Tog da taw? . . ." (p. 164). Transposed this reads: "What did need? Knott. What had got? Knott. Was cup full? Pah! But did need? Perhaps not. But had got? Know not." (The orthography has been corrected as logic suggests.) Watt gets Knott, which is what he needs. Is his cup now full? He doesn't know what he has "got." Much of the fourth stage of his stay in Mr. Knott's house escapes Watt, and thus remains unknown to Sam as well.

The next passage is characterized by a simultaneous reversal of the words in the sentence and the sentences in the paragraph. This text must now be read backward word for word. The passage can be decoded, but the reader who expects to learn more secrets about Mr. Knott will be disappointed. Mr. Knott obviously makes himself *totally* inaccessible, and nothing can be done to please him. The corrected passage reads as follows:

> Shave, he'd say. When had got things ready to shave, the bowl, the brush, the powder, the razor, the soap, the sponge, the towel, the water, No, he'd say. Wash, he'd say. When had got things ready to wash, the basin, the brush, the glove, the salts, the soap, the sponge, the towel, the water, No, he'd say. Dress, he'd say. When

had got things ready to dress, the coat, the drawers, the shirt, the shoes, the socks, the trousers, the vest, the waistcoat, No, he'd say. (P. 167)

After the "fifth stage" on the second floor of the house has passed and Watt has become accustomed to it, we read (in corrected form):

So lived, for time. Not sad, not gay. Not awake, not asleep. Not alive, not dead. Not body, not spirit. Not Watt, not Knott. Daylight came, to go.

The original text is almost unreadable:

Lit yad mac, ot og. Ton taw, ton tonk. Ton dob, ton trips. Ton vila, ton deda. Ton kawa, ton pelsa. Ton das, ton yag. Os devil, rof mitt. (P. 167)

The last reversal is even more complete. Watt begins to simultaneously reverse the letters in the word, the words in the sentence, and the sentences in the paragraph: "Dis yb dis, nem owt. Yad la, tin fo trap . . ." (p. 168). Rearranged this reads:

Side by side, two men. All day, part of night. Dumb numb, blind. Knott looks at Watt. No. Watt looks at Knott. No. Watt talks to Knott? No. Knott talks to Watt? No. Watt then did us do? Nix, nix, nix. Part of night, all day. Two men, side by side.

(Much correction of the orthography is necessary to make the passage readable.)

The passage refers to Sam and Watt, who are marching "side by side" through Mr. Knott's property in a close embrace, the one moving forward, the other backward. I asked Beckett about this passage because it is also possible that it refers to Watt and Mr. Knott; he confirmed that in fact it deals with Watt and Sam.[99]

Sam needs some time to get used to this situation, as can well be imagined. "Much of interest" was thus lost to him during the seventh stage of the closing period in Mr. Knott's house as well.

But this is not the end yet. In one and the same paragraph Watt changes, in rapid sequence, the order of words in the sentence, then the order of the letters in the word, then the order of both the sentences and the letters, and so forth, so that the resulting sounds are unintelligible "Irish" to Sam. Thus much of the eighth stage is also lost to him.

Finally, the situation is reduced to a series of question marks. As Sam grows accustomed to these sounds, however, his hearing itself fails, even though, as he remarks, his myopia remains stationary.

The theme of backward thinking and backward speaking (or backward hearing, for Sam hears Watt speaking these words) is thus brought to a close. Although the results are not satisfying for Sam, he is able to observe, "My purely mental faculties . . . were if possible more vigorous than ever" (p. 169).

The narrative takes a new turn, the scene shifting now to the garden where Mr. Knott, Watt, Arthur (Watt's successor on the ground floor), and Mr. Graves, the gardener, have gathered. Watt, it is reported, is sitting on a mound, while Mr. Knott is moving slowly about, disappearing now behind a bush, emerging now from behind another. Although it is not expressly mentioned, Mr. Knott then disappears into a tree, from which it is said later that he descends.

Arthur uses this gathering as the occasion for telling *his* story; it takes up twenty-eight pages and consumes a considerable amount of reading time as well as space. Because Arthur has only recently arrived in Mr. Knott's house, it is no

99. Letter from Beckett dated April 12, 1978 from Paris.

doubt correct to see his story as a flashback of his past life. But from now on, these reminiscences occur as a result of being in Mr. Knott's garden. Watt listens attentively, but he is happy when Arthur has had enough of storytelling. The story is amusingly introduced with a reference to "Bando," a universal cure-all which Arthur has had occasion to use successfully on himself. The bulk of the story consists of a kind of accounting problem, that is, a dauntingly meticulous description of the process by which individual members of a committee exchange glances with each other. It is one of the longest series.

This scene is interesting with regard to the arrangement of the characters. Watt is sitting on a mound as he listens to Arthur, while Mr. Knott has taken his place in a tree (which suggests Yggdrasil, the great ash tree of Germanic mythology whose roots and branches extend from one end of the universe to the other). An interpretation of Arthur's life story should therefore take this setting into account. Yet Arthur ends his story (his life?) not only out of fatigue, but also, as it is stated, out of desire to return to Mr. Knott's house:

> For there was no place, but only there where Mr Knott was, whose peculiar properties, having first thrust forth, with such a thrust, called back so soon, with such a call. (P. 199)

The region in which Mr. Knott lives thus has the power to call back, immediately and urgently, anyone who has been forced away from it. Mr. Knott's house is a refuge.

This episode is followed by another of Watt's attempts to describe Mr. Knott's peculiar nature, his indefinable appearance, his impenetrable being. But this again is only anthropomorphic insolence on Watt's part. His powers are not equal to the job. Mr. Knott's domestic establishment also forms the object of a series at this point.

Watt's tearful departure from the house is mentioned. Mr. Knott's "singing" is described, and Watt is less able to understand it than ever. Watt wonders at the end how Mr. Knott will manage without him. The formal end of this section is Watt's return backward through the hole in the fence to his own pavilion. Thus ends the account of Watt's experiences in this region.

The structure of part III is therefore quite complicated, but there is no doubt that it does connect directly with the preceding part II. Part III also obviously takes place on Mr. Knott's property, even though this does not appear to be so at first, for Mr. Knott's property does not consist simply of a house, but rather of a house and garden. In spite of the enormous proliferation of images and events, the third part of *Watt* is nevertheless a self-contained whole. This is evident from the way in which the chapter begins and ends. Part III begins with the pavilions and ends with the same image. Watt moves backward to his pavilion and thus becomes separate again from Sam, who remains behind.

At the end of the second part we expected Watt to ascend to the upper floor. Instead, a quite different change of locale is described: Watt is "moved" into another pavilion, into a new house of his own, separate from Sam who only now appears as an independent figure in the narrative. It is stated that the entire story of Watt is told to Sam.

It would be logical to expect that Watt's external and internal horizons, his realm of experience, would be expanded by the move from the lower floor to the upper. But obviously this upper floor is quite different in nature from anything Watt was able to imagine beforehand. The upper floor is much "madder" than he expected. Life unfolds there as if in a maze or madhouse. Thus it was necessary for both the narrative structure and the entire system of imagery to change, so that Watt's own confusion could confront the reader directly through the narrative style. This change of scene demonstrates the precision with which Beckett is able to integrate form and content. The change in the experiential world is correlated with an almost total transformation of the environment, where ordinary relationships are upended. In place of the various rooms on the second floor we find a series of gardens with pavilions for all of the inhabitants. At one point, all the characters are gathered together in Mr. Knott's garden. Although Watt has separated himself from Sam, the two still "communicate" with each other in a highly peculiar fashion.

Much in *Watt* is clearly absurd, but nowhere does the absurd confront us so directly as in this third part. Although it appears that virtually everything has been cut loose from its moorings, we are never asked to accept total nonsense. As soon as the image of the ascent from the lower region to the upper region of the house is exhausted, Beckett simply chooses a new image, and the presence of Mr. Knott becomes more complex and multidimensional. Because Mr. Knott now appears more frequently, he can be approached more closely, even though he is always withdrawing from his surroundings and servants. Nowhere in *Watt* is there a more concentrated attempt to describe Mr. Knott in all his peculiarities; nowhere is the narrator hotter on his trail. But transformation is Mr. Knott's nature—he constantly eludes Watt's grasp. Neither his clothing and appearance nor his living habits can be defined precisely. Although the attempt to obtain intimate knowledge of Mr. Knott ultimately fails, we still learn a good deal about him. Part III is dedicated to him, the unknowable Mr. Knott; he thus becomes the most important element, the climactic point, of the novel. We learn at the same time that our language, especially its logical content, is not equal to the task of describing him. Even imagery fails; metaphors remain incomplete and imprecise. Mr. Knott disappears secretly as Arthur tells his story. Only after it has ended do the branches move as Mr. Knott slides down from the tree. He returns to the house with Watt trailing behind.

Mr. Knott's residence, his property, thus encompasses several regions: the house with its ground floor and second floor, the garden (in which not only he but also his servants move about), and finally the tree (into which only Mr. Knott himself can withdraw for a time). Is the garden intended as an image of paradise, with the tree of knowledge of good and evil in the center—the garden to which those once ejected exert every effort to return? There is certainly an element of parable here, in spite of the absurdities. The oddities, however, are probably more evident to the unprepared reader than the gnosiological aspect concealed behind them.

Beginning and End: Parts I and IV

It has already been said that parts I and IV are related to the extent that one describes Watt's outward journey, the other his return. It remains now to discuss the structure of these two parts and how they relate to each other.

Aside from the narrative frame with Mr. Hackett, which characterizes the situation and corresponds to the conclusion when the railroad employees and travelers stare at Watt as he lies on the ground, Watt's real story begins with his arrival at the train station. There he bumps into a porter wheeling a milk can, and then starts the journey which takes him to Mr. Knott's house. He crosses the threshold of the house without knowing how he has done so. He puts down his bags and removes his hat (which he plays with for a while); then Arsene gives him a "declaration," that is, a preview of what awaits him in Mr. Knott's house. The structure of this first part of the story has remarkable clarity, once it is realized that the narrative frame does not focus on the theme, but simply sets the mood and serves to introduce Watt.

What the novel presents is described quite concretely, without digression or commentary. One point after another is made, and thus moved into the field of awareness. Prior to this, none of the human beings or objects seems to have existed at all; their existence begins only when they are named—the corner around which Mr. Hackett turns, the bench, the lovers, the married couple, and so forth. In the same way, Watt emerges from the depths of the unconscious, is described, increases in clarity, and finally adopts the role assigned to him as main character. (When Sam splits off from him later, Watt is still the one who tells him the whole story.)

An evening mood prevails in the first part. When Watt first appears it is almost dark. The journey to Mr. Knott's house then consists of two sections, the train ride and the foot journey. While on the train Watt is subjected to Mr. Spiro's religious sophistries, and while on foot to Lady McCann's attack—she throws a stone at him which knocks off his hat. This foot journey is interrupted when Watt lies down at the edge of the road and rolls into a ditch. Watt covers the remaining distance to Mr. Knott's house alone and in the dark.

After his preliminary remark about the arrangement of the four parts of the novel, Beckett begins part IV by stating that Watt leaves now *as he came*, that is, in the night. As he was at the end of the first part, Watt is in the kitchen of Mr. Knott's house. Micks, the new man, is sitting there, just as Watt had before: "One moment I was out, and the next I was in" (p. 216). Thus the experiences of the two men are similar—neither knows how he managed to cross the threshold.

Watt's departure is next. Again he is wearing his hat and carrying his bags as he walks down the avenue and then along the road. His clothes are more than comical. They are thrown together at random and are totally inappropriate. (Although it is summer, he is wearing an old winter coat.) Watt arrives at the train station, finds it closed, is let into the waiting room, and spends the rest of the night there. Morning comes. Then follows the rough treatment—the blow on the head and the bucket of cold, slimy water—and Watt's purchase of a ticket as the bystanders look on with interest. Finally the train departs, presumably with Watt on it.

Parts I and IV are thus mirror images of one another. There are narrative frames at the beginning and the very end of the novel. At the beginning it is evening; at the end, morning. In each case there is a walk to the train station, where an accident occurs preceding the actual beginning of the train trip: in part I Watt bumps into the porter, and in part IV it is also a porter who slams the door in his face and (together with the stationmaster) tips the bucket of water over him. Whereas at the end of part I Watt's predecessor gives him a "declaration," it is said in part IV that Watt neglected to say any words of farewell to the new arrival, as he should have done, "The few simple words at parting, that mean so much, to him who stays, to him who goes" (p. 222). These parting words would have corresponded to Arsene's declaration on Watt's arrival.

Parts I and IV correspond in their reverse sequence of events, because Watt's outward journey corresponds to his return. Thus, not only in terms of the narrower narrative frame in which other figures talk *about* Watt, but also in terms of Watt's journey to Mr. Knott's house (including the train trip) and his return, it can be said that these two parts together form a situational frame for the two central chapters (parts II and III).

The structure of the whole definitely suggests a symphony in four movements: I, Introduction and Preview; II, Residence in Mr. Knott's House (ground floor and garden); III, Residence in Mr. Knott's House's Upper Regions (everything appearing greatly transformed or in the process of transformation); IV, Return Journey.

In contrast to other critics, I do not consider the addenda an independent part of the novel, as important as these notes are. The name *addenda* itself precludes this. In view of the importance I attribute to this novel of Beckett's, one sentence from the addenda is worthy of note: "Further peculiarities of this soul-landscape were . . ." (p. 249). Now it is not the further peculiarities—such as warm climate, and so forth—that are of interest, but rather the expression "soul-landscape," for this points out the special nature of Mr. Knott's house and garden where Watt was a temporary resident.

The various entries in the addenda suggest that Beckett

might well have said a good deal more about Mr. Knott's region, the climate of soul prevailing there, and so forth. This can be interpreted as indicating the incomplete character of the book. Watt is not an omniscient narrator. He is a seeker in the labyrinth, an everyman on a strange journey of discovery—a journey for which he is not properly prepared.

The Underlying Gnosiological Aspect of Watt

The only possible spiritual development is in the sense of depth . . . art is the apotheosis of solitude.
      Samuel Beckett[100]

IV

100. *Proust*, p. 46.

The Destruction of Rational Structures: The Condition for Expanding the Range of Experience

Supplementing the plot summary presented in chapter 2, the foregoing discussion of the general structure of the novel— that is, its division into four large parts, the structural correlation between two sets of internally related parts, and difficult to understand but important formal peculiarities such as the inversions and the seemingly endless series—has provided us with indications of what is to be extracted from the whole as the *gnosiological aspect* of *Watt*.

A review of the secondary literature on *Watt* immediately reveals how difficult Beckett can be to read. It is obvious that the author has not given us the "blowlamp" we need to open the sealed box his novel represents. As shown in chapter 1, several critics have produced worthwhile analyses, both of *Watt*'s satirical content and its formal structure. However, although several of them suspect something serious is behind the obvious nonsense, it seems to me that in general they fail to understand the central importance of the "nought" which is the source of everything.

It is unlikely that we can find a solution to *Watt* as long as we deal only with its formal problems or the fictional aspect of its content. That is, we must not overlook the additional capacity of Beckett's fiction to convey philosophical insight or psychological truth. Only when we seek meaning deep enough, in an existential realm beyond subjectivity, can we arrive at a clearer understanding of the implications of the overall structure and absurd elements of Watt's story. It is Watt's "fate," his personal experience, that is ultimately the central problem of the novel.

Ruby Cohn recognized as early as 1962 that Beckett had apparently presented in *Watt* a "suprarational man" in the context of an "irrational world."[101] There is no doubt that the rational plane quickly gives way to an irrational plane of ex-

---

101. *Samuel Beckett: The Comic Gamut*, p. 68.

perience, insofar as the narrative frame can be considered to embody rational events (such as references to Dublin, its streetcars, its surroundings). In reality we are in the midst of absurdity from the very beginning, for who in a rational world responds to a pair of lovers in the manner of Mr. Hackett, and what traveler buys a ticket simply "to the end of the line" (the near, far, thick, or thin end)? Nor is it sufficient to see *Watt* as merely a comical and sarcastic book—although there may well be readers who are completely satisfied with such a view—even though it is true that in its brilliance and richness of variation the humor in *Watt* far surpasses that in any of Beckett's other novels (including *Murphy*).[102]

John J. Mood and other critics have attempted to define the philosophical content of *Watt*. Mood believes that Beckett wanted to settle accounts with rational Western philosophy, but he also maintains that this is not a full explanation of Beckett.[103] He therefore cites Heidegger, whose existential philosophy appears to him to be more to the point. Reason, often considered the ultimate authority in philosophy, is not suitable for describing the irrational (although we need it nonetheless). Heidegger says that the irrational is only the reverse side of the rational, but Mood points out that this metaphor of flipping a coin is inappropriate in the case of *Watt* because there the entire monetary system is bankrupt. This interpretation is correct to the extent that Beckett *temporarily* invalidates the currency, but it errs in that Beckett does not destroy rational structures permanently. Mood asserts, however, "In *Watt*, Beckett portrays this bankruptcy of reason in relation to both the external and the internal world in another way"—that is, with the goal of constructing *his own*

102. See H. Hobson, "The First Night of *Waiting for Godot*," in *Beckett at 60: A Festschrift*, p. 25. According to Hobson, *Waiting for Godot* gave intimations of its deeper meaning at its very first performance, although many responded to it simply as a fascinating and entertaining play. Hobson writes of a "musical experience," the play "touching chords deeper than can be reached by reason, and saying things beyond the grasp of logic."

103. See " 'The Personal System,' " pp. 255ff.

system from the wreckage. As for this "personal system," what value can it have?

There is no doubt that Beckett has created his own means of expression, his personal style—a language that has passed through nothingness, as he says. But does this mean a language that describes nothingness *as* a nothingness? Is the result of this effort mere subjectivism? The term "personal system" awakens this suspicion.

Mood quotes Beckett's remark, "It is the shape that matters" (p. 263); this means, first of all, that Beckett loves the *form* of ideas. We know, for example, that Beckett admires a statement of Augustine, which he uses in *Waiting for Godot:* "Do not despair: one of the thieves was saved. Do not presume: one of the thieves was damned."[104] Occasionally Beckett adds that the shape of ideas intrigues him, even though he might not believe in them. In this way Beckett indicates that a linguistic formulation can be of interest to him, even if he is indifferent to its content; that is, form is more important to him than content. This independence of artistic form from its content of truth (or even the "correctness" of the statement) is definitely characteristic of Beckett and obligates the reader to take a stand. Beckett confirms this explicitly in the preface to his film script: after an elucidation of Berkeley's dictum "esse est percipi" he writes, "The above will have no truth value attached to it, but is regarded as of structural and dramatic convenience."[105]

Must we conclude from this that Beckett has no interest in the content of ideas—he, of whom it is said that form and content are identical? In his book *Samuel Beckett: A Study of His Novels,* Eugene Webb arrives at exactly the opposite conclusion:

> Skilful as he is with language, however, for Beckett language is less important than thought. Most of the

104. See Esslin, *Theatre of the Absurd*, p. 32.
105. Beckett, *Film* (New York, 1969), p. 11.

changes that have taken place in Beckett's language from the time of *More Pricks than Kicks* to that of *How It Is* have been for the sake of more adequately conforming his expression to his thought. It is ironic that a writer for whom thought is so important should have as his message the untrustworthiness of human intelligence or of any meaningful pattern the human mind might think it can discover in the universe. Beckett told Tom Driver, "I am not a philosopher". He probably meant that he held no allegiance to any system of thought, equally distrusting them all. But he is a thinker, and if a person whose entire body of work is a sort of prolegomenon to any future philosophy can be considered a philosopher, then Beckett is precisely that, at least in the sense that he is a man who has explored the limits of thought."[106]

Perhaps we can agree with this much of Webb's assessment, that is, that Beckett is a thinker without allegiance to any system who adapts his mental processes to whatever plane of reality interests him.

Beckett has not always developed his own, original (e.g., dramatic) forms. He has also made use of existing structures. This is not so striking in his prose writings as in his plays.[107] But this is no reason to subscribe to the view that he chooses his structural or formal elements randomly or "merely" according to formalistic criteria. For him, as for many other artists, form is the means by which his deepest and most personal "vision" of reality can be concentrated and expressed. The statement "It is the shape that matters" is typical of an artist.

It is quite a different matter to say whether or not what is presented—the content—can be generalized, and whether it is intelligible and applicable to the average person. But is

106. (London, 1970), p. 19.

107. See Konrad Schoell, "The Chain and the Circle: A Structural Comparison of *Waiting for Godot* and *Endgame*," *Modern Drama* 11 (1968):48–53.

the transmission of information or a "message" really one of Beckett's concerns? Is Beckett, who resists making statements about himself, especially in regard to his allegiances, trying to sell us an idea?

Just as there is nothing arbitrary in Beckett's structures or forms, so, too, there is nothing accidental about his ideas, regardless of whether he borrows them from others (as in the case of Berkeley) or creates them himself. All the same, his meaning frequently does not reside in the external or informative plane, nor in the rational-intelligible content, but rather in a stratum that uses ideas as tools of the imagination to point to deeper relationships. The final "statement" is thus what he makes out of his materials, that is, the work of art itself.

Beckett leaves it to the initiative of the reader or spectator (the patrons of "cafés du commerce," members of churches or universities, as the case may be) to interpret these "statements," but their meaning will be disclosed only as the result of an effort to perceive the work itself without prejudice, to situate it in the total oeuvre, and to relate it carefully to one's own experience. To perceive what is there is indispensable to an understanding of the work, for the work of art becomes a concrete reality only in the act of perception.[108]

Beckett is not Brecht. He does not see himself as a teacher or philosopher (as Sartre did), but he is intensely interested in existential questions. Truths which can be dredged up only from the deepest layers of the personality do not improve by being preached or parroted. In the case of genuinely profound truths, it is possible only to point them out and thus awaken a consciousness of the problems they involve. Truths speak best for themselves.

The first question is, what is Beckett pointing to when

---

108. See Iser, *The Act of Reading*, p. 20. Iser continues: "The text itself simply offers 'schematized aspects' through which the subject matter of the work can be produced, while the actual production takes place through an act of concretization" (pp. 20–21).

he destroys, that is, abandons, our conventional world and accustomed perceptions of reality? What is the point of his search for new forms of expression? Can it be in his own interest to create an entirely private system? To think this would be to underestimate Beckett.

Josephine Jacobson and William Mueller are close to this problem, in *The Testament of Samuel Beckett*, when they write that "his essential poetic mode, his epistemological sense of the relationship between the human consciousness and the world of space and time"[109] is what is really central to Beckett.[110]

Sam observes at one point that "cracks soon appear" in one of Watt's hypotheses.[111] Generalizing this statement, which undermines the foundations of Watt's entire, allegedly "personal" system, John J. Mood applies it in his study of *Watt* to the system Beckett has constructed and finds that it, too, is flawed:[112] "We can now begin to see that the very self which is examining all the other cracks and slips, the very self-constructing rational system, is itself flawed. And that may well be the real mess of which Beckett speaks as being 'all around us' and which Watt describes as 'trouble in (my) mind.' "[113] Mood concludes, "*Watt* has portrayed the equal

109. (London, 1966), p. 11.

110. See M. Hutchinson, "All the Livelong Way," in *Beckett at 60: A Festschrift*, p. 93. Hutchinson cites Shelley's "Prometheus Unbound" (1820) to characterize the depth in Beckett:

> To the deep, to the deep
> > Down, down!
> Through the shades to sleep,
> Through the cloudy strife
> Of Death and of Life,
> Through the veil and the bar
> Of things that seem and are
> Even to the steps of the remotest throne
> > Down, down!

111. *Watt*, p. 148.

112. Mood, " 'The Personal System,' " pp. 255–65.

113. Ibid., p. 264.

failure of rationality to provide an internal system of any validity or use."[114]

It is unlikely that Beckett would have pursued such a superficial plan of destroying the rational world, simply to replace it by a "personal system" that is just as defective. This would have represented a net gain of zero. The breakdown of the external world occurs over the course of Watt's experiences and is a necessary preparation for the breakthrough to the profound dimensions that are of interest to Beckett. Beckett leads our customary (and usually superficial) logic *ad absurdum* because he is describing *what is*. If even what we call normal reality is for Beckett full of absurdity, how much more difficult it must be to describe the irrational reality in which we live when we dream, for example. Nor does our rational awareness extend into the regions from which the human soul originates when a person is born or to which it goes when he dies. Beckett is concerned with finding a means of expression that can encompass these regions as well. "We are such stuff as dreams are made on; and our little life is rounded with a sleep," as Shakespeare says in *The Tempest*.[115]

The destruction of rational structures is therefore not an end in itself; rather, it is an inner necessity. If the irrational, the flawed, and the defective dominate large portions of *Watt*—and Mood rightly points out that about a third of the novel is dedicated to pseudological analysis—this has nothing to do with philosophical dispute or a settling of accounts. Beckett invalidates "Western rationalism," if at all, only on a certain plane of reality. Otherwise, he would himself be insane.

Aside from this fundamental error, Mood contributes much of value to our knowledge of the formal aspects of *Watt*. He analyzes the series with their omissions and "intentional errors," and plots them with meticulous care. François Martel has also done this in a more strictly mathematical way and

114. Ibid.
115. Act 4, sc. 1, lines 156–58.

has provided an impressive analysis of the formal interplay in *Watt*.[116]

With regard to the structure of the novel as a whole, however, these two critics are more or less groping in the dark, because they consider only its formal aspects in detail. This is obvious from Mood's comment that "fully a third of the novel consists of material apparently only distantly related to the rest of the book. Even if one grants a relation, it is apparently a tenuous one, the material being largely irrelevant and repetitious."[117]

A convincing case can also be made for the opposite position that not a single word in *Watt* is superfluous. The meaning of passages occasionally referred to as tedious or boring can be found only in an understanding of the whole.

Most critics have no idea of what to do with the reshuffled sequence that Beckett provides at the beginning of part IV, although it seems as though the author intends to convey something important. John Chalker, who deals with the satirical aspects of *Watt*, interprets it as an expression of the collapse of structure: "The formal implications have to do with the collapse of structure which makes the experience of reading *Watt* so strange and even at times unnerving."[118]

Beckett's rearrangement of the sequence elicits Chalker's comment that "this clearly proclaimed order is not the order of the book, which proceeds rather: one, two, four, three." Thus Chalker believes that he is free to introduce a third arrangement with impunity, simply because the structure, in his opinion, has collapsed.

When Beckett creates a new, "authentic" order at the beginning of part IV, it is obvious that we have been given something to think about. *Watt* as a whole is not simply a "satirical image" of failure, as Chalker apparently believes.[119]

116. "Jeux formels dans *Watt*," pp. 153–75.
117. " 'The Personal System,' " p. 257.
118. "The Satiric Shape of *Watt*," pp. 21ff.
119. Ibid., p. 29.

Eleanor Swanson's reference to *Watt*'s "broken time structure,"[120] which is expressed in the revision of the sequence of parts, is pertinent, but not simply in the sense that the normal sequence of events is *destroyed*. We are dealing here with a deeper problem—the escape from time. John J. Mood writes: "*Watt* is divided into five parts: four numbered sections and a final brief eight-page conclusion entitled 'Addenda.' These sections follow neither a chronological order nor the order in which they were related by Watt to Sam, the narrator."[121]

Beckett suggests a new arrangement of the four parts of the novel. This suggestion is not designed to break up a chronology, which was never a fixed frame of reference in the first place. Like Sterne, who in *Tristram Shandy* abandoned chronological progression in favor of an associative process,[122] Beckett does not slavishly watch the clock. It is generally believed that Beckett abandons both the normal sequence of time and the normal plane of experience in *Watt*. To do this he has had to abandon rational forms, or, if you will, to "destroy" them. The point over which opinion now divides is whether the destruction of the world of rational ideas makes it possible to obtain a meaningful insight into the "irrational," or whether the result of this revolution in consciousness means chaos, meaninglessness, and madness. Most critics are of the latter opinion, at least as far as Watt (the narrator) is concerned, but also usually in regard to Sam. For this reason they set the scene of part III in an insane asylum (although it must be admitted that Beckett's choice of imagery strongly encourages this tendency as well).[123]

---

120. "Samuel Beckett's *Watt*," pp. 264–68.

121. " 'The Personal System,' " p. 256.

122. See Gerd Rohmann, ed., *Laurence Sterne* (Darmstadt, 1980).

123. David Hesla speaks of Watt and Sam as "intimates at a mental institution" ("The Shape of Chaos," p. 87), and Ann Trivisonno calls Sam a "lunatic narrator" or "lunatic creator" ("Meaning and Function of the Quest," pp. 28–38). The return to normal existence is justified by Trivisonno on for-

In spite of the madhouse atmosphere, critics agree that not only is the "Kafkaesque" world that Watt enters described with formal brilliance, but also that the content of that world is presented convincingly in all its flawed fragility. If there were no meaning at all in what Beckett says about Watt or in what he has Watt say, there would then be hardly any dispute among the critics who have spent so much time studying this work.

Beckett proceeds step by step. First he has Mr. Hackett (the name "echoes 'Beckett' "[124]) and his interlocutors, Mr. and Mrs. Nixon, have their say; then he has Watt appear, who makes his train journey and finally arrives at Mr. Knott's house on foot. Watt's stay on the ground floor, after crossing the threshold, begins at that point and in part II it becomes the subject of the hero's own account of his experiences. Then comes the break. Part III shows us the split between Watt and Sam, their time together, and finally their return to their respective pavilions. The final image—the mingling and separation of the smoke from the two houses—refers to the evanescence of their relationship. This schizophreniclike personality split definitely has much that is grotesque and absurd in it, but this does not necessarily mean it is pathological. Part IV is, in contrast, "normal" again. The proponents of the view that the whole *terminates* in madness will tend to share Chalker's opinion that the parts of the novel must be arranged in the order one, two, four, three.

It must be remembered, however, that the irrational element pervades the entire novel, and that its greater intensity in part III is merely part of a pattern. It is in fact possible to verify an ebb and flow of the irrational over the course of the entire novel, although neither the individual part nor the

---

malistic grounds: "If Watt's journey to the house of Mr. Knott is one in a series of metaphorical quests for a new kind of fiction, it cannot possibly end in the lunatic asylum. Watt must return to the material world of traditional fiction and begin his search anew" (p. 37).

124. See Hesla, "The Shape of Chaos," p. 87.

whole ever returns to the same state in which it began.[125] A return to an identical, original state never occurs in any of Beckett's works. Even when there are apparent repetitions, as in the two acts of *Waiting for Godot*, differences remain between the two occurrences—in the second act, for example, there are a few leaves on the tree that had previously been bare. This clearly indicates a qualitative difference. Watt returns, but as a man who has undergone a change, as a man who has found a way to lighten his load and make room in his "grousebags" for new experiences.

Mathew Winston, whose study has been mentioned above in the review of secondary literature, has pointed out the importance of the blurring of the boundary between subject and object, as is clearly indicated by the first footnote in *Watt*.[126] He believes that the only reason we know anything about Watt at all is that Sam has created him. It is stated in the novel that Sam is the source of all our information, but that he has merely been writing down what Watt has dictated to him. If Watt has no reality of his own, however, as might perhaps be assumed, then he is merely the reflection of Sam's mind or personality. This train of thought is logical. But who is Sam? Regardless of whether Beckett is referring to himself as Sam (which is likely, since this is what he is called by his friends), he is in any case Sam's creator and thus stands behind the narrator. That he has Sam record the story that Watt allegedly tells him, however, perhaps reinforces the view that the author identifies with Sam. This identification does not mean, however, that everything in the novel other than Sam is *only* invention. Winston believes, for example, that if Watt as a character is an invention of Sam, then Mr. Knott is also pure invention. This is true only to the extent that the author is obviously the inventor of all his characters. Beckett, as the

125. Hesla writes, "each of the chapters returns the reader to more or less the same world it carried him from" (ibid., p. 102).
126. "*Watt*'s First Footnote," especially p. 80.

author of the fiction, is the creator of Watt, Sam, Mr. Knott, and everyone else who appears.

Whether or not Mr. Knott and Watt are real remains unaffected by this. In a narrower sense, therefore, what Beckett wants to express through these characters, why he describes (invents, shapes) them in the first place, is still unanswered. The use of several different narrators in a series is a standard procedure in modern fiction, and Beckett himself uses this technique in his trilogy (*Molloy, Moran,* and *Malone*). Secondary characters such as Arsene, Arthur, and Micks play brief roles as narrators in *Watt,* their changes in identity being associated with a change in point of view or even with a change in the plane of reality on which the narration occurs. Watt himself, however, occupies a special position. He passes (or is conducted by the author) through the very different spheres of the four parts of the novel, and therefore undergoes the most extensive changes (metamorphoses), up to and including a split in consciousness. The change of protagonists in earlier works (e.g., from Belaqua Shua to Murphy) cannot be said to be meaningless either, but it occurs as part of a still traditional narrative structure.

Everything would still be nonsense if the purpose of the novel were simply to tell the story of a mentally ill person— the story of a lunatic committed to the same mental institution as the fictional author, Sam. In other words, the novel would be meaningless if the destruction of the rational world were to bring about only lunacy, if there were nothing suprarational to succeed the rational. This "irrational" element, which nonetheless has meaning, must be searched for. There must be some kind of reality that corresponds to the new form of existence through which Watt passes. If that is the case, *Watt* is no longer the story of a lunatic, no longer mere fiction, but rather Beckett's faithful account of his experience of another reality. Literature does indeed deal with such experiences. In *The Act of Creation* Arthur Koestler writes, "Literature begins with the telling of a tale . . . The events thus represented are mental events in the narrator's mind."[127] This is certainly pertinent to *Watt*, but it does not answer the question of what is really happening: What *are* the mental events in Beckett's mind that are being represented? Is what is described real, or is it mere contrivance, fantasy, a form of misdirection, or even of mental illness?

More cautiously we can also say this: only if *Watt* is a work of art that has reference to reality or that extends beyond the subjectivity of the artist (which gives the work its "color") is it in fact a work of permanent value, because then it points the way to that suprarational and simultaneously suprapersonal sphere. It then has gnosiological value because it expands our horizon of experience into a world otherwise closed to us.

Mathew Winston expresses the opinion that Sam fulfills four functions: he participates in Watt's experiences; he retells the story which Watt has told or whispered to him; he is the writer of the book *Watt;* and finally, he comments on the happenings in the book, for example, by providing footnotes or stepping out of the plot in some other way. A lunatic would hardly be capable of this.

We cannot overlook the fact, however, that as a first-person narrator Sam does not appear at all until part III, and neither Watt nor Sam are present in the very beginning of the novel. This suggests again that Beckett stands behind the whole as author, which is in fact self-evident; it is he who divides up the action and directs it; it is he who introduces the characters, makes use of them for a time, and dismisses them (like Mr. Hackett). But he takes Watt seriously. Watt remains the main character from the moment of his appearance. Sam splits off from Watt. We could, of course, also say that Watt moves out of Sam's pavilion as Watt enters into his own sphere, his private pavilion with garden. The two remain in touch, however, remaining apart only for limited periods. In spite of their separation, they cling together.

127. (London, 1964), p. 301.

What does this move to the separate pavilion, this "split," mean in terms of content? This mirror image/two-in-oneness of Watt and Sam is one of the great ideas of the novel and constitutes one of its most essential formative principles. At the moment when it was necessary to separate Watt from Sam (or vice versa), Beckett could perhaps have also spoken of Watt I and Watt II, perhaps even of a "lower" and "higher" self. It is evident, however, that he didn't mind loaning his own name to *one* component of this main character. To this extent he identifies with Watt. We can correctly assume that the author's own consciousness is split, for only in this way would it have been possible for him to adopt and describe the opposite states of mind of Watt and Sam, which are, to some extent, mutually exclusive. Watt and Sam inhabit two different regions of a distinct world, and in their progress toward each other, each represents the mirror image of the other.[128]

When we look at the manner in which Beckett describes this world, we can, without approaching Beckett too closely, speak of a didactic treatise, albeit a thorny one. *Watt* does not simply entertain us with its irrational and absurd narration; on the contrary, it also shows us the way to the proper sphere of this irrational element. To paraphrase Beckett, we can say that *Watt* is *nothing less* than a game, for games of this sort relate directly to reality. The game involving Watt (and Sam) deals with a split of consciousness that is not madness. *Watt* is an investigation of the laws of the spiritual world, a world which can be entered only if the usually inflexible human consciousness can adapt to it—by splitting.

The Imagery Used To Express the Being and Becoming of Man

I now proceed to discuss the inner content of *Watt* and thus pass beyond the points developed up to now; at this point,

128. Ionesco also describes a mirror-image world in *Le pieton de l'air* (see n. 98).

then, it would be wise to recall Beckett's warning at the end of the novel, "No symbols where none intended" (p. 255). The German and French editions convey even more urgent warnings, promising dire consequences to anyone who sees symbols in the text.

This warning is definitely to be taken seriously. All the same, it should not be understood as an absolute prohibition against reflecting on whether or not this work of art, *Watt*, has any meaning or value beyond that as an image of madness. It does not prohibit, for example, reflection on the extent to which *Watt*'s content is accessible only in images, as is proper in literary texts, nor on the extent to which this content transcends the face value of the imagery and points to a reality that can be grasped only through a deeper response to the language. Thus, it is not our intention here to skim the cream off the top, for which Beckett reproached the readers of James Joyce;[129] on the contrary, we will attempt to grasp the *condition humaine* with which Beckett confronts us and out of which he has created this novel. If we succeed, we shall find that the access to *Watt* is not blocked but opened.[130]

The re-creation of the novel in our imagination can, on the simplest level, consist of responding to the imagery as a naïve reader would; at the other extreme, the immanent content is recreated within the reader's mind in collaboration with the author, a process for which the term "objective re-creation" might perhaps be used. This latter form of reception consists of analysis followed by synthesis. The first impression is supported and supplemented by intellectual reflection. The content of experience is processed, examined for its ratio-

129. See "Dante . . . Bruno. Vico .,. . Joyce," in *Our Exagmination Round His Factification for Incamination of Work in Progress* (Paris, 1929), p. 13.

130. Hesla's position has my full approval, namely, that it is one of the chief dangers of interpretation (e.g., of Mr. Knott) "that it can initiate an explication of the novel as an allegory in the traditional sense." And, ". . . there is far too much in the novel which cannot be accounted for by reference to a neat allegorical system" (Hesla, "The Shape of Chaos," pp. 101–2).

nal content, and placed into a meaningful arrangement which transcends the level of image perception. If it is a symbol, the image is not the final destination. The point is to grasp the entire system of meaning which has been conveyed, even if it has been conveyed through images.

R. L. Brett writes, "*Image* and *imagery* . . . refer to any use of language that depends on concrete particulars rather than abstractions."[131] The characteristic of the symbol, however, is to refer to something beyond itself; this has already been discussed in the first chapter. A re-creation that is not exhausted in the mere (naïve) absorption of images by the mind but instead is a mental acquisition, leads to a justifiable *interpretation* or is at least an attempt at an active interpretation. Depending on the kinds of private experience that enter into the process, this effort can either bring us close to or keep us far away from the "meaning" that the artist himself, consciously or unconsciously, has given the work. Obviously there is art whose intellectual content is such that it will be considered "meaningless" by the observer. Regardless of actual artistic quality, this can be the fault of the observer or of the work itself. Only if the work is realistic in the traditional sense of the term (pertaining only to externals, not as a stylistic element in the context, for example, of a grotesque tale) does reception require no individual effort; the meaning is obvious. This is so because our consciousness is, from the very beginning, adapted to the external world.

If art does not in fact merely "copy" but also reveals or discloses something, then that which is to be learned must be found or grasped as the result of a process of discovery. This is what is accomplished in the process of re-creation. If imaginatively heightened language is involved, as it is in Beckett's case, then the problem is to learn to read the metaphorical language of literature and to understand the higher-level reality which is thus conveyed.[132] All this should be obvious.

131. *An Introduction to English Studies* (London, 1965), p. 22.
132. See Smuda, *Becketts Prosa als Metasprache*.

When Beckett warns against an all too facile or overly superficial interpretation, he does so because he lives on the plane of the poetic reality he describes in his fiction and because he experiences it fully. At the same time, he expects his readers to experience it as well. Often enough, an intellectually prefabricated "meaning" is erected in front of direct poetic expression and its implications. This construct prevents the work from speaking to us directly. Such an interpretive approach robs a work of art of its profundity.[133]

There is really no argument against a careful re-creation of imagery, including its rhythmic and musical components so characteristic of the metaphorical language of a work such as *Watt*; nor can any serious objection be raised against an interpretation of a work based on such a re-creation. This is part of a response that strives to see what is actually presented and to come to terms with what is there; it is also part of the effort to become aware of the content in its multidimensional complexity. This is not an arbitrary act, nor does it involve the mistake of reading into the text something which is not there.

Beckett's style can be described as "direct." This reflects the directness of his experience. Thus, directness of expression, the denotative element, brevity, and precision also characterize his "visions." The task of chapter 3 was to make us aware of these elements, embedded as they are in the text, and to discuss the composition and certain formal features of *Watt*. Now the matter at hand is to deal with the individual images themselves.

In *Watt* we find an inquiry into the very nature of human existence that is not afraid to enter areas inaccessible to rational thought. Watt personifies the question of the multidimensional nature of man and the passage of the human soul through birth and death. Just as sleep represents an altered state of consciousness, birth and death represent even more radical forms of the changes of consciousness which the human soul must undergo. Watt undergoes these transfor-

133. See again Iser, *The Act of Reading*, pp. 4ff.

mations and describes this experience as accurately as he can, and despite the fact that he is not an initiate, but only a man, Beckett still chooses him as an object worthy of interest.

On earth Watt struggles forlornly, carrying his baggage wherever he goes. He has many debts to pay to the world around him—not just the five shillings or the six and nine-pence. He is a poor wretch, down on his luck, at the end of his rope.

Watt begins each of his journeys at the railway station, both at the beginning of the novel and after his departure from Mr. Knott's house. It is clear that the introductory nar-rative frame is not by accident a roundabout discussion of pregnancy and birth. It begins with a love scene on a bench under the close observation of Mr. Hackett. It proceeds with a pregnant woman passing by, and this is logically followed by the story of how Mrs. Nixon (Tetty) unceremoniously thrust her son Larry into the midst of life, giving birth to him during a party at her house. We are not told this just for the sake of entertainment; it is necessary as an introduction to one of the central themes of the novel that all existence is misery, and birth, which ushers in a life of inevitable suffering, is itself a lamentable event. This is expressed, for example, by Mr. Hackett's crippled body, his loneliness, and his miserable fate, resulting from his fall from a ladder while abandoned or neglected as a child by his parents. Even before Watt appears, the reader is given a full picture of Beckett's own attitude to life.[134]

134. Jacobsen and Mueller point out the same situation: "Man begins, for Beckett, not only with the unretractable fact of birth, but with the fact that his birth, the misery of life, and the desirability of death are many and various." And, "Beckett's many remarks on birth—and conception—are hardly cheerful" (*Testament of Samuel Beckett*, p. 111).

On the occasion of the death of his newly born son, Gotthold Ephraim Lessing (1729–1781) expressed a similar feeling in a letter to his friend Esch-enburg (dated December 31, 1777) from Wolfenbüttel, which he wrote while his wife was dying in childbed: "How I hated to lose him, this son! For he had so much sense! So much sense! I know what I am saying. Was it not sensible that he had to be pulled into the world with iron tongs? That he so

Watt appears, but we do not learn how he actually arrives at the station. There he collides with a porter, who is wheeling milkcans about. It might appear farfetched, but a little familiarity with Beckett's imagery suggests that this is the moment of Watt's birth; that is, his journey in the train begins after he has had this rather violent meeting with the porter and his milkcans. Because birth is a punishment (and a relatively nasty business as well) and motherhood thankless drudgery, consisting in part of lugging around milkcans, we can conclude that it is necessary for Watt to undergo this "trauma" before he can start his life's journey. The sophistry he hears from Mr. Spiro obviously represents part of his education, even though Watt finds it meaningless. He has to leave the train abruptly. He hikes to Mr. Knott's house, but on the way there, after Lady McCann has attacked him, he suffers a fainting spell and literally rolls into a ditch—or into the grave—where he hears a mixed choir (of angels?) sing. He lies there for a time, face down. Watt then arrives at the house; it appears at first to be locked tight, but after a brief search he manages to get inside—he *crosses the threshold* (of death) but does not know how he has done so. The same thing happens to Arthur later.[135] In the house, the fire in the grate is burning out; Watt takes off his hat to cover the lamp so that he can see the ashes glow.[136]

---

quickly noticed the sorry state of things? Was it not sensible that he seized the first opportunity to take leave of it again?" (See the facsimile of *Zwei Briefe Lessings über den Tod Eva Königs* [Wolfenbüttel: Herzog August Bibliothek, n.d.]). For the sake of the section quoted here, I brought Samuel Beckett the facsimile of these letters with me to Berlin on February 22, 1975.

135. Referring to death as a "crossing of a threshold" (from here to the "beyond") is a conventional expression. In this context, the "threshold to the spiritual world" is also mentioned. (See Rudolf Steiner, *Rudolf Steiner Gesamtausgabe*, vol. 206 [Dornach bei Basel].)

136. Watt's behavior in casting shadows on the wall, and so forth, recalls Plato's cave allegory—the shadowlike nature of ideas. That Watt uses his hat to do this is no coincidence; the stone thrown by Lady McCann strikes his hat and knocks it to the ground. (Without a hat, Lucky in *Waiting for Godot* cannot think.)

The organization of Mr. Knott's household is hierarchical: when one person goes, another comes. Watt listens to Arsene's statement. There are therefore servants (on different floors) and a master (as in heaven). After being introduced by Arsene, Watt begins his life in the "beyond," and this is the central part of the novel. At first, Watt's experiences can be communicated after a fashion, that is, put in a narrative form which makes sense (part II). This changes when he moves upstairs.

On the ground floor, Watt must perform relatively menial services; he must dispose of the garbage, prepare the food for Mr. Knott's meals (whoever he is, he is the master), and bring the meals to him. During this period, Watt learns to accustom himself to the new reality in which he must live. For example, he must get used to the fact that the logical relationships which were self-evident on earth no longer apply. The "reality" in this realm, as the visit by the Galls demonstrates, is different. At first, this world can be described only in images, but their sequence has no external logic. Time has changed its character also, and memory alone determines Watt's thought processes. Watt's account of his surroundings is vague; the rapidity of his speech is conspicuous, as is the eccentricity of his syntax. All this points the way toward the next plane of experience where the problems of expression are even greater (part III). For Watt, the time has come to create something out of nothing—something which acquires the character of reality only through speech (thought). Here the danger of anthropomorphizing is confronted also. We must remember Beckett's admonition, "Every word is a lie." The descriptions are in danger of becoming so vague and inexact as to be totally uninformative. The right words cannot be found. Circumlocutions take the place of direct expression, and although these circumlocutions appear to be manifestations of insanity, they are merely absurd because they are not what we expect. The difficulties of saying what is meant give rise to the series of stuttering starts and restarts, to the desperate adoption of a new set of images to replace a set that has reached its limits. In this world, everything is in intimidating motion, for here reality can no longer be conveyed with static concepts:

> To such an extent is this true, that one is sometimes tempted to wonder, with reference to two or even three incidents related by Watt as separate and distinct, if they are not in reality the same incident, variously interpreted. (P. 78)

> The state in which Watt found himself resisted formulation in a way no state had ever done, in which Watt had ever found himself. (P. 81)

Nevertheless, Watt accustoms himself to his "loss of being." He adjusts by attempting to expand his ability to perceive.

Many images, such as rats, recur. Far from being bothered by the rats, Watt considers them his particular friends; they give him joy. After he and Sam have fed an especially plump young rat to the other rats (in part III), they have the feeling of being very close to God. This grotesque observation, which even has something repellent about it, can be understood only by interpreting the rats, not as living animals, but rather as "gnawing" or nagging thoughts and memories, intellectual monsters (concepts, perceptions), which at a certain moment are thrown to each other to be consumed or annihilated. It would be nonsensical to abandon at precisely this point our sensitivity to imagery and to employ aesthetic standards that are not necessarily applicable.

Watt, in company with Sam, does not feel part of the new reality until he succeeds in throwing the rats to each other, that is, until he can hold them in check or destroy them. Corresponding rat images occur in other novels of Beckett. In *How It Is*, Beckett speaks of the past as the "little rat" hot on the heels of a man, and "the unnamable" asks himself whether he could perhaps avoid being gnawed by a fat old rat by talking in order to say nothing. Is this the exorcism of memories? In *Watt* this game with rats is not carried to a definite end, but it does go so far as that "feeling" of being nearest to God.

Other motifs are simpler to understand, such as the bags, which are always set down whenever Watt enters the "beyond" (where he is permitted to lay down the burden of his earthly experiences), and the hat (certainly a derby). These are "poetic truths," symbols of reality of the language of imagery. The text must be read closely. For example, the bags that Watt picks up again as he leaves Mr. Knott's house are far from empty. There is already (or still) something in them, even though he is setting out on a new journey, the next "hunt." The derby is evidently associated with the powers of the mind (as in the slapstick comedy *Waiting for Godot*); and it is useful to remember that the patterns on which our minds operate always tend to be "old hat." Just as one of the functions of a hat is to protect the head from falling objects, our mental processes (on earth) serve to shield and individuate us. This bears some relationship to rituals, such as that in Catholicism that requires women to keep their heads covered in church. There are also the gestures involved with being self-aware and contained or in ecstasy ("being beside oneself"). Lucky pursues his thoughts until his hat is knocked off; Lady McCann's attack (she is a pious, militant lady) is directed at Watt's hat.

And the dogs? As far as Mr. Knott is concerned, they are not much different from the Lynch family itself, the primary concern of its members being to procreate. The family consists solely of wretched creatures whose services are required from time to time to get rid of the garbage. Whole communities of hungry dogs and people are maintained for this purpose. The approach is thoroughly sarcastic, a strong persiflage of the grotesque misery of these dependents.[137]

137. "Most of Beckett's mirthless laughs are directed against physical deformity, against the process of elimination and eating, against loathsome and even pathetic sexual practices. Virtually all of his characters are deformed in one way or another, and no family in the history of literature suffers so

There is much talk of being spared or not spared in connection with the Lynch family. Both the living and the unborn can be "spared." The living are spared the misery of life by dying (as the forty-year-old Liz is relieved of her misery by dying after giving birth to her twentieth child); others are spared the even greater misery of being born. This is only logical.

Before Watt moves up to the second floor, we learn about Erskine, who has been serving Mr. Knott on the second floor before Watt's advancement. Erskine is a nervous sort, always rushing up and down the stairs. Watt is curious about him and tries to discover what is in Erskine's room.

A remarkable picture is hanging there, with a circle open at the bottom and a blue spot—a moving, dynamic picture, it is said, a circle and its center in search of each other, in boundless space, in endless time (i.e., beyond space and time).

This is an image for both the entire book and the place Watt has now reached. The picture or painting is an integral component of Mr. Knott's household, as Watt establishes after tedious and laborious deliberation.

Everything is "a coming and a going"—this realization is termed a "tenth grade xenia," which sounds comical but which is probably meant in all seriousness. *Watt* deals with the search of a center for its circumference, of the self for its spiritual home, its authentic milieu. And Watt finally does get to see Mr. Knott and to become increasingly interested in penetrating beyond his continuously changing appearance to the underlying essence. He is now ready for the move to the second floor. This region in Mr. Knott's house can be described only by a perceiving consciousness that has split in two, and even under these conditions the results are far from satisfactory. Watt is aware of his failure.[138]

---

many fascinating variations of deformity as the Lynches" (Jacobsen and Mueller, *Testament of Samuel Beckett*, p. 100).

138. Rudolf Steiner also describes a "dissociation" of the members

It should not be imagined that Beckett provides us with a complete tour through the realm of the spirit in *Watt*. Nevertheless, the essential features of this plane of reality are presented in outline form. The primary element is the reversal of relationships. This does not imply the destruction of linear, cause-and-effect logic, for this has already been taken ad absurdum, first in Arsene's summary of his stay in Mr. Knott's house and then in Watt's own account of his period of employment on the ground floor. The laws that govern Mr. Knott's house are those of the world of imagination or of inspiration and intuition, and the mental images, sounds, words, and so on, taken from the ordinary world convey to us only the shadows of that other world.

From Watt's very first moment in Mr. Knott's house he is no longer on an earthly plane. Watt no longer suffers under his earthly burdens, and he devotes himself more and more to the service of Mr. Knott. He is relieved here of the trials (such as putting on clothes) to which he was previously—and again later—subjected. But the problems of communication and understanding are considerable. Watt, because he is not very advanced in the spiritual life, necessarily encounters great difficulties in Mr. Knott's house.

Watt would have preferred to be left alone in his own

(*Wesensglieder*) of man as a precondition for "extrasensory perception." The normal configuration of ego, the soul (the so-called astral body), and the life forces (the etheric body), whose separation from the physical body occurs only in death, can be brought about in exceptional cases by *conscious* effort in the form of a "going apart" (as in sleep), which leads to the ability to see into the spiritual world. This power of vision is described in three variants: imagination (consciousness of images), inspiration (the hearing of spiritual messages), and a state of intuition (the highest form of insight into the spiritual world). For details, see Rudolf Steiner's basic writings, *Theosophy, Occult Science*, etc.; these are nos. 9 and 13 respectively of the *Rudolf Steiner Gesamtausgabe* (Dornach bei Basel), also available in English. Further details can be found in the ten lectures Steiner gave in 1913 at The Hague: "Welche Bedeutung hat die Okkulte Entwicklung des Menschen für seine Hüllen–physischer Leib, Ätherleib, Astralleib—und sein Selbst?" in no. 145 of the Steiner *Gesamtausgabe*.

pavilion; never, never did he wish to leave it. But this is a resolve to which he gives only lip service and to which he cannot hold fast. Watt must move on; he must move out of his new domicile. To communicate with Sam a bridge first had to be repaired, and someone had to tear holes in the fence with great force. The weather must be favorable—there must be sunshine (clarity) and wind (pneuma) for the two to come together. Undergrowth prevents freedom of movement, as it does in many other works by Beckett.[139]

Watt injures himself on the fence and bleeds. For a moment, the "ecce homo" image is apparent. This is the place where the fat young rat is finally eaten by the other rats. Watt and Sam are together at this moment; they are one (after an "exchange of views"). What could appear to be blasphemy acquires quite a different aspect when seen in this light. The two are nearest to God at such moments, because they have destroyed all their earthly memories and mental images. But this state does not last long. The meeting of Watt and Sam can only be temporary.

The motifs of walking (or crawling) backward and speaking backward have already been discussed with numerous examples in chapter 3. It should be pointed out, however, that some people have had the experience at the moment of death (or near-death) of watching a film of their lives running backward at high speed.[140] Rudolf Steiner, who has studied these phenomena as part of his spiritual science, associates this with the "loosening" or incipient separation of the soul (the astral body) from the life forces (the etheric body) which begins at the moment of death. (Thus the images of memory are contained in the etheric body). The inversion of reality, which occurs elsewhere in literature as an image of penetrating through to a world behind a mirror, belongs to our traditional imagery of passing into the next life. Just as dying, as a

139. See Samuel Beckett, *Stories and Texts for Nothing* (New York, 1967), p. 75.

140. See Raymond A. Moody, *Leben nach dem Tod* (Reinbek bei Hamburg, 1977).

bodily process, takes time before the moment of death arrives, initiating the inversion of relationships, life after death also has a temporal structure, although this can only be inferred.[141]

The precondition for spiritual perception is the elimination of external sense perceptions. Some of this "housecleaning" is accomplished in *Watt* by means of the (incomplete) logical series. The suprarational is also glimpsed in the games with mathematical images, such as that with irrational numbers or in the example of extracting the roots. Severe demands are made on the reader's imagination. The results are often unsatisfactory because the description can never get beyond the level of approximation.

Mr. Knott is and remains for Watt a remote being on a clearly distinct plane, although Watt is allowed to follow him into his house. Mr. Knott's "aura" is described in such a way that Watt sees his situation less, rather than more, clearly. Despite his further progress, Watt retains anthropomorphic ideas of what Mr. Knott really is. Watt even suspects that Mr. Knott can exist only as long as there are witnesses to his "not needing." But this conjecture falls from Watt's lips in a manner "halting" and "faint with dubiety" (p. 203).

Toward the end of part III, Mr. Knott apparently disappears from view. Watt can still hear his singing, but it has become weaker and more monotonous. He scarcely understands the meaning of the picture in his room any longer (formerly Erskine's room). His consciousness of the spiritual world diminishes; the time is coming when he must leave the "circle" (i.e., his spiritual home centered in the cosmos) through the opening at the nadir. Watt is about to return to the railway station.

For Mr. Knott's house and garden are not the final stop on Watt's journey. The daily fluctuation in Mr. Knott's belching and other forms of behavior is certainly not an unintentional reference to the Greek philosopher Heraclitus's dictum "everything flows." In *Waiting for Godot* Beckett paraphrases

141. See Johannes Hemleben, *Jenseits* (Reinbek bei Hamburg, 1975).

Heraclitus with typical lack of respect in Estragon's remark, "It's never the same pus from one second to the next."[142]

We have yet to consider *how* Watt returns to the realm of the living and *why* he bothers to return at all. No explanation is given for the fact that he leaves Mr. Knott's house and walks to the station. His time is simply up. He sits in the kitchen; the milk sours; he smokes a cheap cigar to the end. His time in Mr. Knott's house is over. We don't know why, but a new man comes, and that must suffice.

The traditional view or hope is that after death an eternal life begins in the next world. A more and more widespread belief today is that death represents the end of everything. But this idea has gained currency only in the present age of materialism; in the past, most people were convinced of a life after death. In Christianity, the resurrection of the dead at the Last Judgment is considered an article of faith. Less prominent in Western consciousness is the idea of reincarnation, which is not as foreign to Christendom as some defenders of the faith like to think. Its denial seems to function as part of their effort to set Christianity apart from theosophical groups and Eastern religions.[143] Rudolf Steiner's anthroposophy, for example, considers reincarnation a spiritual reality.[144]

At the beginning of part IV, Watt is ready to leave Mr. Knott's house. He walks down the avenue, illuminated by the moon and other heavenly bodies. They cast

> a light so strong, so pure, so steady and so white, that his progress, though painful, and uncertain, was less painful, less uncertain, than he had apprehended, when setting out. (P. 223)

---

142. *Waiting for Godot,* act 2, p. 39.

143. See Emil Bock, *Wiederholte Erdenleben: Die Wiederverkörperungs-idee in der deutschen Geistesgeschichte* (Stuttgart, 1932 and 1952); and G. Wiedemann, *Gedanken über die Unsterblichkeit als Wiederholung des Erdenlebens* (Stuttgart, 1961).

144. See Rudolf Steiner, *Reinkarnation und Karma* (Stuttgart, 1961).

Watt's appearance this time, described previously in detail, suggests the full measure of misery to which he is returning. This is the point at which the "grey air aswirl with vain entelechies" that waft around Watt like shadows is spoken of. Watt picks up his bags again, still three-quarters empty, and proceeds to the station.

Beckett makes several attempts to describe the period of intrauterine life that now follows. First, Watt's posture is described: a yearning for rest and warmth overcomes him; he stoops and wants to lay his arms on the table and to bury his head in his arms, perhaps to dream of dives from dreadful heights into rocky waters.

> So he stooped, but he did not stoop far, for hardly had the stoop begun, when it ended, . . . when he checked it, and remained fixed, in an aggravation of his semi-upright station, a situation so lamentable that he remarked it . . . Inwardly he was diverted, to be sure, and for an instant his mind turned off from care, but less than if he had had the force to smile, or outright to laugh. (P. 222)

After Watt arrives at the station, as he looks back in the direction of Mr. Knott's house, his attention is arrested by the sight of an unusually large, inelegant figure, a woman or nun, or even a priest. It is wearing a long seamless garment, which looks like a sheet, and this creature of indeterminate sex is wearing on its head something like a "depressed, inverted chamberpot." In his state of deepest darkness, Watt suddenly notes the flashing and disappearance of the words, "The only cure is diet." Watt's concern is not, however, with what the figure in reality *is*, but rather with what the figure in reality *appears* to be, and it is remarked, "For since when were Watt's concerns with what things were, in reality?" (p. 226).[145]

145. The question of this shapeless figure's meaning is not easy to answer. The most plausible idea to me is that it has to do with an intimation of the etheric body, which is formed as a "gestalt" and is incorporated into

Having thus arrived at the station, Watt spends the rest of the night in the waiting room, which is sealed off at both ends. This scene represents an accurate image of life in the womb.

Horst Breuer devotes an entire chapter of his book to the "return to the womb" in Beckett's works.[146] In reference to *Watt*, however, he comes to no definitive conclusions. Watt's journey passes through the stages of both birth and death and is therefore, according to Breuer, not compatible with a yearning to return to the womb. This is the view, I believe, espoused by critics who approach the topic of intrauterine life in Beckett with conventional psychological concepts. Even Breuer points out only the generally known fact that an intra-uterine posture is frequently suggested in Beckett's works—in *More Pricks Than Kicks, Waiting for Godot, How It Is, Imagination Dead Imagine, Ping, Murphy,* and of course in *Watt*. In *Molloy* Beckett goes so far as to play on prenatal memories.

Before he is let into the waiting room, Watt lies down on a seat, puts his hat over his face, and concentrates on the problem of vision: the eyes open in the dark! Watt hears voices whispering in his skull like a "patter of mice." This patter might well represent the first stirring in his brain. His thoughts also turn to excretory matters. All this clearly suggests growth in the womb and a dreamlike awareness of the reawakening of bodily functions. Mr. Case comes with his storm lantern. Watt gets up and tries to preserve his balance. He also notices that the waiting room is devoid of furniture—there is only the floor, walls, and ceiling. Later he perceives that there is, after all, one object, which turns out to be a high, narrow, black wooden "chair" fastened to the floor at one of its legs—the placenta. But first, Watt has the impression, while he is drooping "sigmoidal in its midst," that this is a waiting room "of which even the nicest degrees of the

---

the soul. See Steiner, *Gesamtausgabe*, vol. 9, where there is a discussion of the embodiment of soul and spirit.

146. *Die Kunst der Paradoxie*, pp. 72ff.

strange and usual could not be affirmed . . ." (p. 233). We should remember that the embryo is in fact curled up in the shape of a sigma in the uterus, facing backwards; that is, it is suspended from its umbilical cord (downward from "above"), and the placenta, so to speak, is its "chair."

It would be difficult to find another explanation for this description of Watt's position. The image of the "object of some importance" that does not belong to the ceiling, wall, or floor similarly fits only the placenta. Furthermore, Watt smells an unpleasant odor, which he believes to be coming through the floor. If Watt is in the womb, this odor must be coming from the mother's rectum or anus, located behind or below the uterus. Watt is almost compelled to put down his bags and take out his handkerchief, or, more precisely, his roll of toilet paper.

It is therefore obvious that the imagery used to describe this place, this waiting room in the railway station before the start of Watt's new journey, can be understood only as an embodiment of life in the womb. Watt must pass through this period of waiting before he can be released to "freedom."

Ejection from the uterus follows. This is known to involve some discomfort. Watt is too close to the waiting room door and is struck on the head by it as it is flung open. He is knocked to the floor and lies there stunned. Some railway employees pour water—later to be mixed with blood, the pail having fallen and struck him—over his face to bring him to life. "Now I am at liberty, said Watt, I am free to come and go, as I please" (p. 238).

"Poor fellow," says Mr. Gorman, the stationmaster. "Help him to rise" (p. 238). A gap in the manuscript follows (presumably a hiatus in Watt's consciousness), and Mr. Gorman insists that they cannot leave Watt lying there like that. As Mr. Nolan runs to fetch the bucket, Watt hears fragments of Hölderlin's poem "Hyperions Schicksalslied," a song which fills him at this "moment of destiny."

The birth process is accompanied, as it so often is, by coarse remarks from the bystanders. "Is that the gob?" asks

Mr. Nolan. "Or is it a hole in his trousers? (pp. 239–40). At this point, he and Mr. Gorman tip the bucket of slimy water over Watt, but not before Mr. Gorman has spit emphatically into the bucket. The question of the "gob" or "hole" is obviously a reference to the uncertainty as to whether the baby (Watt) is being born head-first or bottom-first. Other characters appear, notably the infamous Lady McCann (whom Mr. Gorman has just wished to hell). We recall that it was she who followed Watt on his way to Mr. Knott's house and knocked off his hat with a stone.

As in *Waiting for Godot,* a breathless boy arrives as a messenger from "Mr. Cole," who obviously is the master of the trains. Mr. Cole protests that his trains have not been able to get through, that they have been held up by the signalman. Lady McCann, who has no idea who Mr. Cole is, sends the boy back to his master to tell him that the station has been the scene of "terrible events" (namely, Watt's birth), but that now all is well (p. 243). There are definite grounds for suspecting here that "Mr. Cole" is only a cover name for Mr. Knott. The name "Cole" suggests "cool," which expresses the aloofness of this gentleman. Mr. Cole (alias Mr. Knott) as the distant and unapproachable master of the trains (or life journeys) complains about the delay caused by the improperly placed signals. He communicates with those involved, but (like Godot) only through a messenger (angel). The parodistic character of this description of the birth process is unmistakable, as are its implications.

Mr. Case appears again and wipes some of the slime from Watt's face. Although he does not recognize the face, the clothing appears to him to be the same as Watt's. When Watt finally stands up, to the considerable diversion of Mr. Gorman and the others, the stationmaster asks him, "Who the devil are you . . . and what the hell do you want?" (p. 243)—a question every newborn baby might well expect to hear. In this case it is directed to Watt.

We know how the novel ends: Watt buys a ticket and his new life journey begins. He is enroute to some unknown, distant goal. "All the same, said Mr Gorman, life isn't such a bad old bugger" (p. 245).

The Psychological Situation of Watt and His Creator

The discussion of *Watt* presented up to this point raises two questions. First, there is the question of the psychological origins of this work. This is directed at the inner biographical situation of Beckett himself, insofar as it is reflected in the figure he created.

Second, we must inquire into the meaning of the problems presented in *Watt* for us as anthropologically oriented readers. The subjective element of a work of fiction can easily awaken the interest of readers. It gives the work a personal character and color. This originality is part of the greatness of a work of art; on occasion, it alone constitutes its greatness and importance. But there are works through which we learn something new in reference to our own lives as human beings because they disclose or discover something universally valid. *Watt* can be considered a work of art of this latter type.

To answer the first question we must rely on Beckett's text and his occasional statements. In regard to *Watt*, this has already been covered in the preceding sections. Much could be added by going back to *Murphy*. Beckett's works succeed each other chronologically, but in addition each novel represents a further stage of development over the preceding one. Eric P. Levy builds his argument on this assumption.[147]

Like all important fiction, Beckett's narratives exhibit certain situations typical of their historical context. The conscious involvement with the existential issues raised by *Murphy, Watt, Mercier and Camier,* and the trilogy can lead the reader to an independent response to these issues and to a more aware spiritual life. This in turn is probably associated

---

147. *Beckett and the Voice of Species: A Study of the Prose Fiction* (Totowa, N.J., and Dublin, 1980).

with the fact that these issues have been formulated out of the deepest level of Beckett's inner life.[148]

In the following discussion we will turn our attention first to *Murphy,* because it describes the initial psychological state out of which not only *Murphy* but the entire series of the following works arise. In this way we can take a further step toward discovery of gnosiological undercurrents. It is my primary purpose to show which meaning Beckett's work possesses with respect to man's spiritual condition (or calamity) in our time.

In the early 1960s Martin Esslin wrote, "Beckett's entire work can be seen as a search for the reality that lies behind mere reasoning in conceptual terms."[149] *Behind* this conceptual reasoning there is concealed a world which contains not only subjective elements but also a "suprarational reality" which deserves our interest. Because we are in the position of forming at least approximately correct ideas about this hidden reality (as in mathematics, where we can also define what irrational numbers are), it might be better to discard Esslin's phrase "reasoning in conceptual terms" and talk instead about "rational understanding," for it is in the region beyond such an understanding that what concerns us here takes place.

In the previous chapter it was shown that Beckett's world of experience can be evaluated properly only by means of a specifically learned imaginative power of mind, because Beckett's text itself is imagistic in nature. He who attempts to penetrate these regions will tend to describe them initially as twilight zones or zones of darkness, in contrast to the rational light of our waking consciousness, our intellectual life. This need not stand in our way. It is also not a certainty that "imagistic thinking" alone can provide a complete understanding of the character of these worlds.

The novel *Murphy* and the novel *Watt* were written in succession, but in addition, the character Watt is a direct suc-

148. See chapter 1, pp. 29ff.
149. *Theatre of the Absurd,* p. 64.

cessor to the character Murphy. Watt has been given a new name because he represents a further stage of development. He is a metamorphosis of Murphy. If this were not the case, he would not have deserved another name. As Klaus Birkenhauer has shown, this is also clearly evident from a stylistic comparison of *Murphy* and *Watt*.[150]

Whereas *Murphy* still reveals a certain delight in eloquence, is elegant and ingratiating, and impresses and enchants the reader with euphonious words, in *Watt* Beckett abandons such rhetorical and literary ornamentation almost completely. That is, he is developing the unmistakable "Beckett style," which in its concise, sober manner suggests pure denotation and achieves its effect through relentless denial. Nothing that might have been suggested to the author by virtue of his personal history, that is, unconsciously, is allowed to enter into this style.

This depersonalizing tendency is already clearly evident in *Watt*, which was written in English. In addition, the ties to immediate experience of the external world, such as the conditions of life in London which can still be found in *Murphy*, have disappeared.[151]

In certain parts, *Watt* is already similar to the *Texts for Nothing*. In these texts, Beckett's language creates the peculiar impression of disembodiment, even though it is full of concrete situations and images. But it is also characterized by fractures and jumps; constantly interrupted by stop-for-breath commas, it gropes searchingly forward, step by step. Here is a sentence from the beginning of these *Texts for Nothing:* "The top, very flat, of a mountain, no, a hill, but so wild, so wild, enough."[152] This is the type of prose we find in *Watt*. Through perseverance, in spite of the repeated interruptions, some

150. *Beckett*, pp. 70ff.

151. In response to the remark that in *Murphy*, in contrast to his later works, he had used a number of biographical elements, Beckett answered: "Yes, that is true, especially in regard to the localities in London, which I knew very well" (conversation with Beckett on April 12, 1969 in Ussy).

152. *Stories and Texts for Nothing*, p. 75.

progress is nevertheless made. Language thus embarks on a voyage of discovery. Klaus Birkenhauer believes that the function of this language is to help the speaker create himself, but it does even more, for in a certain sense it assumes the existence of the speaker and proceeds from there *to find a new reality.*

Beckett's series of protagonists on this voyage continues from Murphy to Watt or Sam, then to Molloy, Moran, and Malone, and finally to the Unnamable, the end point of this line of development. This series can also be traced back to the figure of Belaqua Shua.[153] Starting from this figure, who initiated the role of observer, we can see a process of profound change in the narrative point of view. Iser has described this change: "The Beckett trilogy is based on an extraordinary paradox. The novels show how it becomes increasingly impossible for their narrators to conceive themselves—i.e., to find their own identity; and yet at the same time it is precisely this impossibility that leads them actually to discover something of their own reality."[154] Iser then quotes a sentence of Merleau-Ponty that aptly describes this existential situation: "The absolute contact of the ego with itself, which is the identity of being and appearance, cannot be posited but only experienced before any affirmation."

This remark shows us again how difficult it is to recreate Beckett's texts in our imagination. The author not only forces the reader to change his viewpoint now and then by altering the narrative point of view, which is nothing new, but he also forces the reader to empty his mind of all that is external and set aside all his accustomed logical interconnections. Not all readers can or will subject themselves to this process of emptying the mind. Some will stop reading, or will push on to the end only for formal reasons and never experience the depth required of them. In principle, Beckett antici-

153. See *More Pricks Than Kicks* (London, 1970) and Fletcher, *The Novels of Samuel Beckett*, p. 14.
154. *The Implicit Reader*, p. 174.

pates in *Watt* much of what is fully achieved only in *The Unnamable* at the end of the trilogy—a solitary point of self-discovery. He who must survive without a name is only a "mote" in the darkness.

Iser aptly describes this situation: "It is the distinguishing mark of reality that it resists integration, and the conscious mind turned in upon itself is in a position to discover this truth."[155] The loss of one's name does not imply a loss of the ego or personhood; on the contrary, it strengthens self-awareness. It is an experience of what personal consciousness is in reality.

The question of how this development took place in Beckett himself may be allowed. His confrontations with various alter egos (Belaqua Shua, Murphy, Watt, etc.) occurred over the course of many years, until he reached a state in which the act of naming became impossible, a state in which he knew what it was like to be "unnamable." An echo of this self-discovery is found in Beckett's play *Not I* for a voice (a mouth) and a listener draped in a white garment.[156]

Beckett's *Murphy* was published in 1938. John Fletcher was the first to write of the years Beckett spent in London (1933–35) when this book was conceived;[157] Deirdre Bair has also given us a description of these years.[158] As a young man Beckett lived in Chelsea, and at the invitation of a friend, who happened to be a physician, he visited the Bethlehem Royal Hospital, a psychiatric institute in Beckenham near London. Here is where he is supposed to have gotten the idea for *Murphy*. Beckett has admitted that *Murphy* contains more biographical details than his later works, but it is still valid to say that the essential aspect of *Murphy* cannot be traced to *any* specific set of external experiences, much less to a short visit to a mental hospital. On the contrary, *Murphy* chiefly reflects

155. Ibid., p. 175.
156. Knowlson and Pilling, *Frescoes of the Skull*, p. 195.
157. See *The Novels of Samuel Beckett*, p. 38.
158. *Samuel Beckett* pp. 174ff.

Beckett's internal state at that time, and only to a minor extent his external status as well. In spite of this, Murphy remains Beckett's creation, with all the hallmarks of one of his early protagonists. Murphy is *not* the author himself.[159]

What astonishes the reader in *Murphy*, and what the critics have appreciatively noted, is Beckett's accurate description of the mental state in which he, a young Irishman in London, found himself at that time. It is logical to assume that this "status report" is not mere invention, but rather is a reflection of certain complex inner processes going on in Beckett's mind. This hypothesis can be supported by the fact that Beckett's actual later development—as suggested by the evolution of his main characters—is already foreshadowed in this early work. The clarity with which the young man could differentiate three zones of the spirit, which were then to shape his fundamental attitudes for the rest of his life, remains a source of wonder. For this reason, the secondary literature on Beckett is full of references to the famous passage on the state of "Murphy's mind," even though the description is also full of parodistic elements.

At the beginning of the passage on these three zones of consciousness, we read:

> It is most unfortunate, but the point of this story has been reached where a justification of the expression "Murphy's mind" has to be attempted.[160]

The text that follows deals solely with what Murphy's mind "felt and pictured itself to be," which was, after all, "the gravamen of these informations" (*Murphy*, p. 107). Therefore, if the essential point of the novel, or in parodistic terms its

159. Beckett would not let himself be identified with Murphy. Although he admitted that Murphy's act of tying himself to the swing was a "methodologic gesture," to clear the head, to aid the thinking process, he rejected further questions with the joke, "Murphy is not so silly as to write a book" (conversation in Ussy on April 12, 1969).

160. See Beckett, *Murphy*, pp. 107ff.

"gravamen" (grievance), is Murphy's mental state, then we must appraise it in this light.

Beckett pictures Murphy's mind as a "large, hollow sphere," which is possibly a reference to Leibnitz's monads. To a certain extent, Murphy thus bears solipsistic traits,[161] at least as long as he resides in his own private world of images. The distorted quotation from Spinoza that Beckett places at the beginning of chapter 6 of *Murphy* also points in this direction: "Amor intellectualis quo Murphy se ipsum amat." As John Fletcher points out, the original quotation from Spinoza refers to the "love with which *God* loves himself."[162]

Murphy's dualism—that is, his view of the eternal separation between body and spirit—is then described. It is necessary for Murphy to alternate among states of light, half light, and dark. The point is expressly made that the purpose of this alternation has nothing to do with clarity of vision. The three states imply no value judgments whatever. They could just as well have been described in the reverse order, for they are, after all, stages of contemplation, and it would be possible to speak of a descent or an ascent of the soul with equal validity.

Murphy feels himself split in two, into a body and a spirit, but it is clear that the three zones belong to a purely mental world. Even though the bright, illuminated zone reflects experiences from the physical environment, Murphy's mind processes these images with complete freedom. This is immediately evident from several comical examples of this state: "As he lapsed in body he felt himself coming alive in mind, set free to move amongst its treasures" (*Murphy,*

161. See Alvarez, *Samuel Beckett*, p. 76. Alvarez believes that the worlds which Beckett describes in his novels (at least since *Watt*) are in all cases landscapes of the interior, that Murphy's solipsism was the product of a whim—entertainment for a man with too much education who was bored and irritated by the conventionality and ordinariness of his life. *Watt*, in Alvarez's opinion, is "diffuse," a symptom of a madness which overpowered him.

162. Fletcher, *The Novels of Samuel Beckett*, p. 50.

p. 111). The "treasures" referred to are, of course, the treasures of the imagination.

> There were the three zones, light, half light, dark . . . In the first were the forms with parallel, a radiant abstract of the dog's life, the elements of physical experience available for a new arrangement. Here the pleasure was reprisal, the pleasure of reversing the physical experience. Here the kick that the physical Murphy received, the mental Murphy gave. It was the same kick, but corrected as to direction. (*Murphy*, p. 111)

Murphy, playing with his treasury of images in this zone of light, has his first taste of the inner life. The ability to reverse directions is noteworthy: that which had a specific direction in the physical world occurs here in the opposite direction, but is still under the influence of personal volition.

The second zone is described as that of contemplation, as the renunciation of all external stimuli and the influence of memory. This condition of stillness and concentration requires no "correction." Murphy experiences the "Belacqua bliss" of contemplative self-absorption.

Contemplation thus follows the stage of free association, of unchained reprisal for the pains of physical existence, typically called a "dog's life." This contemplation is noncompetitive; the forms have no parallels. Here Murphy is able to move freely "from one unparalleled beatitude to another" (*Murphy*, p. 112). The third zone, the zone of darkness, contains only forms, but these are constantly changing, immersed in an ongoing process of coming into and passing out of existence—a tumult. Here Murphy is only a "mote" in the darkness of absolute freedom.

This is a highly expressive way of describing consciousness experiencing a reality in which "forms" no longer have any fixed meaning. "He did not move, he was a point in the ceaseless unconditioned generation" (p. 112). Beckett also speaks of a "matrix of surds" (which simply means "nothingness"), the source of spiritual inspiration or the starting point of the not-merely-subjective spiritual experience to which Beckett refers repeatedly thereafter.

When Murphy plunges into this creative chaos, he feels like "a missile without provenance or target, caught up in a tumult of non-Newtonian motion" (p. 112); he is obviously immune to the law of gravity. The sensation of being a tiny mote in this vast dimension of absolute freedom, however, was "so pleasant that pleasant was not the word" (p. 113).

As a novel *Murphy* is similar in many respects to the first zone. Step by step, Beckett emerged from the arbitrariness of this region. The comic style and Irish humor of this early work should not fool us into losing sight of its serious undertone. In this regard *Murphy* resembles James Joyce's *Ulysses*,[163] which is also parody from start to finish. Nevertheless, Joyce's seminal novel analyzes the misadventures of Leopold Bloom and his young friend Stephen Dedalus in a way that demands to be taken seriously. The same can be said of Beckett's Murphy.

A superficial reading of *Watt* also gives a dominant impression of comedy or of this "Irish flavour." There cannot be much objection to a reading of the novel on this conventional literary level, although the reader will fail to recognize the substance which makes these early novels of Beckett into essential components of the entire oeuvre.

Beckett closes chapter 6 of *Murphy* with the sentence, "This painful duty having now been discharged, no further bulletins will be issued" (p. 113). Adhering to his own policy ever since, Beckett has provided virtually no commentary on the mental attitude of any of his later protagonists.

The "Dog's Life" on Earth and the Difficulty of Access to Mr. Knott's World

Peggy Guggenheim, who was in love with Beckett in the 1930s, reported that at that time Beckett was afflicted by ter-

163. Paris, 1922.

rifying memories of being in his mother's womb. He is said to have experienced crises in which he thought he was going to suffocate. She also described him as a fascinating young man, but one who would often sink into apathy.[164] It was common knowledge that, like Belaqua, he occasionally wished to "be back in the caul on my back in the dark forever."[165] Further details on this topic can be found in Horst Breuer's *Samuel Beckett.*[166]

In addition to having terrible memories of life in the womb, Beckett obviously suffered his entire life from the fact of having been born at all. He has made many different statements to this effect. When Elmar Tophoven once jokingly asked Beckett what he had done to deserve the job of translating Beckett texts for more than twenty-five years, the author answered him, half in jest, "That is the sin—being born."[167] In *From an Abandoned Work* we also find the following remark: "No, I regret nothing, all I regret is having been born" (p. 142).

The following passages from *Endgame* are also typical of Beckett's world view. Hamm scolds his old father, Nagg, with the words, "Scoundrel! Why did you engender me?" When Hamm speaks of the time before Clov was born, Clov remarks with a certain ambiguity, "God be with the days!"[168] Hamm speaks of his "sublime" misery with the bitter irony, "Can there be misery—*he yawns*—loftier than mine?"[169]

Beckett makes innumerable references to the "dog's life" on earth. Horst Breuer writes, "For all Beckett's heroes,

164. See Margaret Guggenheim, *Confessions of an Art Addict* (New York, 1960), pp. 48–51. The author confesses that she had been "terribly in love" with Beckett for an entire year, but he refused to commit himself to her in any way.

165. Cited in Esslin, *Theatre of the Absurd*, p. 29.

166. P. 72.

167. This conversation took place in my presence on June 26, 1978 in the PLM Hotel in Paris.

168. Beckett, *Endgame*, pp. 49 and 44 respectively.

169. Ibid, p. 2.

birth was the great catastrophe that marked the start of their unloved life in the world."[170] We should recall that there were two things that Watt could not abide: "one was the moon, and the other was the sun" (p. 33), as we read before he rolls into the ditch. After he has become aware of the "bare hard dark stinking earth" and has begun to climb out of the ditch, two additional things displease him: "one was the earth, and the other was the sky" (p. 36). As he is on his way to Mr. Knott's house, Watt has nothing but disdain for the earth, and later, on the same road on the way back to the station, he breaks out in tears at the necessity of leaving Mr. Knott's vicinity.

It is in no way my intention to confuse Beckett himself with his characters. All the same, it must be kept in mind what Lawrence E. Harvey has written as a footnote in *Samuel Beckett: Poet and Critic* on the relationship between the author and his protagonists in *Watt:* "On the one hand each self is fictional in the deepest sense of the word. Man knows his own being, if it exists, imperfectly at best. His literary creations are phantoms of his imagination, without grounding in reality. Neither Murphy nor Watt is Beckett. On the other hand they resemble each other in too many ways to be thought of as wholly arbitrary."[171] Harvey also describes the various narrative points of view that develop in conjunction with the different protagonists in *Watt.*[172]

None of Beckett's characters can stand his physical body; it is tolerated with extreme antipathy, or at best with stoicism. Many of his characters are cripples, down-and-outers, or handicapped people of one sort or another.

It is obvious that Beckett has transferred his pessimism and intermittent aversion to earthly life to his characters. His personal tranquillity and friendly manner are acquired traits, clearly the product of prolonged inner struggle; he was not by nature gifted with stoicism or equanimity. Deirdre Bair

170. *Samuel Beckett,* p. 75.
171. Lawrence E. Harvey, *Samuel Beckett: Poet and Critic,* pp. 349–50.
172. Ibid., chapter entitled "Watt as Artist and Art in *Watt,*" pp. 373ff.

describes Beckett's difficult years in great detail. One of the many passages she quotes, although without attribution, is highly informative and completely believable: "Optimism is not my way. I shall always be depressed, but what comforts me is the realization that I can now accept this dark side as the commanding side of my personality. In accepting it, I will make it work for me."[173]

Beckett's natural reticence and lack of pretension have been attested to many times.[174] In his younger years he occasionally abandoned his low profile when it conflicted with his other views. For example, he had difficulty restraining his emotions when critics' ignorance of Joyce was involved. His own criticism was then biting and caustic, as the essays "Dante . . . Bruno. Vico . . . Joyce" and *Proust* demonstrate. Perhaps it was his intellectual superiority that made it so difficult for him to remain unassuming. Later he refused to take part in arguments or polemics of any kind.

It is reported that as a young man Beckett was capable of shocking behavior from time to time, primarily when he was drunk. Whether this was out of high spirits or despair cannot be determined from our vantage.

Later there is never any talk of such extravagant behavior—not even in Bair's biography, which would certainly have provided such details if it were possible to do so. Beckett adapted himself to life as well as he could, though never to the point of becoming a conformist. The yearning for a purely spiritual life remained with him, as everything he has ever written shows. His contempt for life has to some extent given way to a milder attitude over the years.

The dualism of Beckett's attitude toward life is also revealed in his contemplative tendency, his yearning for meditative absorption, his need to withdraw, and his pronounced shyness of public exposure. All this suggests a striving for

173. *Samuel Beckett*, p. 352.
174. See Charles Monteith, "A Personal Note," in *Beckett at 60: A Festschrift*, p. 87.

spirituality, which survives outside the framework of organized religion.[175] Intellectual freedom and independence are
Beckett's supreme values.

Readers and spectators often sense this depth in Beckett
and develop an appreciation for his fundamentally elusive
expressiveness. Under the proper conditions, the element of
provocation inherent in his work leads the spectator beyond
the stage of protest to that of self-discovery and assent. Ernst
Schröder, who played Hamm in Beckett's Berlin staging of
Endgame, experienced this "awakening" effect within himself
and has given us a valuable description of it.[176]

It is precisely from confrontation with repeated negation
that the awareness of and desire for personal insight and the
experience of a deeper reality can arise. Wolfgang Iser describes this in his article entitled "The Pattern of Negativity in
Beckett's Prose": "Negativity is the hallmark of the typical
Beckett text. It is produced by a relentless process of negation." Iser describes the effect this produces as "suction":
"Negativity brings into being an endless potentiality . . . It
stimulates communicative and constitutive activities within us
by showing us something is being withheld and by challeng-
ing us to discover what it is."[177]

In face of the emptiness and spiritual aridity of existence, hope is always kept alive in Beckett's characters. The

175. On September 23, 1969 in Berlin, Beckett emphasized that he
always valued the Old and New Testaments, "simply because of the beauty
of the language." He pointed out that Biblical references occur frequently in
his works. His disinterest in the religion is obvious. This outer alienation,
however, needs to be subjected to a more sophisticated set of distinctions in
regard to Beckett's inner attitude to these questions. In regard to *Watt*, Harvey
has devoted an entire chapter of *Samuel Beckett: Poet and Critic*, "The Religious
Dimension," to these problems.

176. "I asked Beckett whether the mighty Hamm might not have a bad
conscience after all. Pause. He looked at me, a bit roguishly, a bit surprised,
and just a little bit pleased. He said softly, 'You think so?' I don't know of
any author or any director who would have answered in this way" ("Proben
mit Beckett," *Frankfurter Allgemeine Zeitung*, November 17, 1967).

177. *The Georgia Review* 29 (1975):706–19.

play goes on. Religiously oriented critics have concluded from this that Beckett wants to say "Credo quia absurdum est." But this is surely not the case. That watching *Godot,* for example, nourishes faith (faith in someday being delivered from misery and desolation) is a fact of audience response which no one denies. But the precision of the dramatic presentation and the hard-edged, uncompromising quality of the writing dispel any illusion that the rest of the job will be easy. There is no opportunity for escape or self-delusion.

An emotional response out of mere belief would be too impoverished. Responses out of religious conviction are not sufficient. Beckett was obviously exposed to enough of this in his youth, and it left him unsatisfied.[178] Any ready-made explanation is meaningless unless, and until, the truth of it, if any, is personally experienced. Beckett's critical faculties are alerted by any sign that truth on this personal level is lacking.[179]

"Waiting for Godot" has not become an often-quoted phrase by accident, for it expresses an expectant attitude typical of our time. The question of the true identity of Godot does not, however, require a fixed answer. For one person Godot is "God" because he expects Him, while for someone else Godot is merely a provider of material necessities. For yet others the name "Godot" stands for the spiritual world (in which Mr. Knott resides), which those who want a deeper understanding of themselves and the world seek to enter, a world to which access is gained by crossing a threshold, as

178. Beckett's parents were Low-Church Protestants. Beckett's mother, a pious woman, was extremely unhappy when she noticed that her son Sam had lost all interest in the church (conversation with Beckett on September 23, 1967).

179. On November 9, 1967, after we had been speaking of Schopenhauer and Eduard von Hartmann, Beckett expressed the thought that no answers are to be found in philosophy either—not even from Hartmann (who introduced the idea of the unconscious). When I mentioned Rudolf Steiner, whom Beckett had only heard of, he wondered if Steiner had perhaps glossed over the difficulties too easily. He listened to my objections without contradiction and said at the end, "I must look into Steiner."

Watt does to enter Mr. Knott's house. Godot is the hope of the "green" beyond the hills—assuming, of course, that it is still green there after all.

Arthur's desire to interrupt his story (which was his life) is based on his desire to be with Mr. Knott again and to dwell in his "haven." Martin Esslin quickly saw that Mr. Knott is similar to the unknown Godot.[180] Both are mysterious, unpredictable, and unapproachable figures. Much is expected of both. Neither one allows himself to be seen as a rule, yet both are a constant presence. They are usually out of sight, for they exist in a different sphere. This is why they make use of messengers to communicate with man, "messengers of the Lord" being simply another word for angels.

At the dress rehearsal for the Berlin production of *Endgame*, which took place under Beckett's direction on March 7, 1975, in the Schiller Theater, the messenger boy, who plays the role of goatherd, appeared very clean and neat—he was simply "angelic." In a conversation during the intermission between the first and second acts, Beckett was asked if this boy shouldn't be a bit dirtier, since he *is* supposed to be a goatherd. Beckett rejected the suggestion vigorously and said in a friendly tone, as if it were self-evident, "He is after all a *messenger*, coming from a totally different sphere." And he repeated, "from a totally different dimension."[181]

Even if we do not want to identify who Mr. Knott (or Monsieur Godot) *really* is, it is obvious that, if he exists, he lives *somewhere else*. Hamm, after his futile attempt to say the

180. Esslin, *Theatre of the Absurd*, p. 18.

181. The question was asked by my wife, Dr. Marie Renate Büttner. The entire conversation was also heard by many others. Among them was an employee of the Herzog August Bibliothek in Wolfenbüttel, who at my request has confirmed Beckett's statement in a letter of July 18, 1979 in the following words: "The best thing is for me to quote to you what I had written down for myself on the following day (after the general rehearsal): . . . Mrs. Büttner told Beckett during the intermission that she had been amazed that the boy had been so clean. Beckett's response: 'But the boy is coming from another world.' "

"Our Father," complains that the "bastard" does not exist, but Clov replies, "Not yet."[182]

We might suspect that Mr. Knott exists only when we imagine him to exist, but this is just as unprovable as the theory that he actually does exist as long as we are not able *to perceive* him. This ambivalence in fact characterizes Watt's situation with respect to Mr. Knott as long as Watt has not penetrated deeply enough into Mr. Knott's sphere.

In *Waiting for Godot,* this waiting for the unknown is played through to the end. Only the two appearances of the messenger, who keeps hope and expectancy alive, actually speak in favor of Godot's real existence—otherwise he would be incapable of dispatching a messenger. For the spectator or reader, Godot will "really" exist only when access has been found to his "residence." For Watt, this approach begins when he crosses the threshold of Mr. Knott's house. But since he had traveled facing backward in the train, because he did not want to see where he was going, this crossing of the threshold occurred without his knowing how it was done.

It remains to be determined how we can grasp or get to know Mr. Knott, wherever he is. If he really does exist, there must be a way of reaching him. This is a problem of "gnosiology."

The Inner World Depicted in Watt *and the Reality to Which It Corresponds*

Moi je suis tout à fait incapable d'en parler. Je ne le vois et ne le vis que du dedans.
    Samuel Beckett[183]

Maurice Maeterlinck, winner of the Nobel Prize for literature in 1911 and one of the fathers of modern drama, characterized

182. Beckett, *Endgame,* p. 55.
183. Letter to me of May 24, 1963. Beckett wrote this to explain his standpoint that it is completely impossible for him to judge the meaning of his works.

his writing as an expression of the "vie intérieure." This pre-occupation with "inner" reality provided him with the following insight: "In fact, the deeper we penetrate into human consciousness, the fewer conflicts we find. And it is possible to penetrate very deeply into a consciousness only when it is extremely clear."[184]

This statement applies to no one more directly than Samuel Beckett. This inner clarity does not mean, however, that Beckett must also serve as his own interpreter. One reason for this is surely that the language of the artist is not the same as that of the critic and that, fundamentally, art requires no "explanation."

Nevertheless, if I join those who, in substantial numbers, have attempted to interpret Beckett's work by publishing my views on *Watt*, I do so as a tribute to Beckett. As I mentioned in the first chapter, such critical studies are the result of the unique qualities of Beckett's work that provoke questions and stimulate interpretation. As Marianne Kesting writes of Beckett's work in a review of Konrad Schoell's *Das Theater Samuel Becketts*, "Its puzzling qualities demand interpretation by the literary critics."[185] Of fundamental interest is Kesting's observation that Beckett "literally cries out for an intellectual analysis and interpretation; but this, given the nature of Beckett's work, would be impossible to accomplish by means of an approach intrinsic to the literature. The entire body of modern aesthetics, philosophy, and the sociology of the arts—the widest possible spectrum of historical and literary data—would have to be brought to bear."

Some of this work has already been done, and there has been no lack of intellectual effort and professional skill. But there still remains considerable doubt as to whether Beckett's work has really been given its due. In many cases, critical discussion which goes beyond a catalog of formal character-

184. "Das Moderne Drama," in *Der Doppelte Garten* (Jena, 1925), p. 68.
185. See "Rätselhafter Samuel Beckett: Der Dichter in den Händen der Literaturwissenschaft," *Frankfurter Allgemeine Zeitung*, October 28, 1968, p. 3L. Kesting also discusses here Fletcher's *Samuel Beckett's Art*.

istics tends to conclude that Beckett's works involve a hermetic discourse between the writer and his own creations. This means, however, that Beckett has nothing more to say to the world than what Murphy, as solipsist, tells us when he uses the "elements of physical experience available for a new arrangement" to provide a "radiant abstract of the dog's life."[186] But even Murphy progresses to the stage of contemplation and thus reaches the void, the "womb of the irrational," and as Beckett admitted in one of his few additional remarks to the "Bulletin" (in *Murphy*), it was his goal to create a poetry which has passed through nothingness and finds a new beginning in another dimension.[187] *Watt* is such a new beginning. Already the preliminary results achieved in this book are impressive.

In the trilogy Beckett continues his journey along the same path. He reduces the "heroes," Moran, Molloy, and Malone, by progressive stages until a virtually immaterial, bodiless, pure consciousness is reached—the nameless and unnamable. At the same time, he switches to first-person narrative, the proper point of view for a novel of consciousness. In the development of these novels and their parts, the first-person narrators are connected in a single line of descent, so that ultimately each of the earlier ones is seen as an embodiment of one mind in search of itself.

On the narrative and situational plane this reduction corresponds to a regression to infancy, a return to the mother's bed (*Molloy*), to increasing immobility (*Malone Dies*), and finally to memberlessness (*The Unnamable*).

Beckett wrote *How It Is* in 1960. As in the trilogy, Beckett presents us with handicapped characters who are capable of only halting progress, but in contrast to the earlier novels, he presents human society as a system of mutual interdependence and master-servant relationships. This novel, whose French title, *Comment c'est,* is identical in sound to the word

186. Beckett, *Murphy,* p. 111.
187. See n. 69.

"commencez," is interpreted by Alfred Alvarez in *Samuel Beckett* as a worm's-eye view of the afterlife: "He can only cope with this unbearable knowledge, like Watt, by page after page of calculation . . . And yet, given Beckett's habitual meticulousness of both style and feeling, given also that some kind of limbo or life-in-death has been the destination of all his efforts, given the terminal depression which really is how it is with him, then the book gathers to itself a certain grandeur. Above all, it is an extraordinary *tour de force* . . . It is the aesthetic equivalent of what scientists call 'pure research.' "[188] Although I cannot agree with many of Alvarez's judgments, these words do say a good deal about the gnosiological side of the work and its author, Beckett.

Beckett gives an accurate account of what the "voices" tell him. There is Watt's voice, for example, which is soft, rapid, and sometimes even unintelligible. It is inconceivable that Beckett has failed to notice that what he is saying could not have arisen out of himself alone, that his soul or spirit is responding to something outside himself which he then is compelled to express in words. After he has destroyed the "maya" of external sensory appearances—first for himself, then for us, his readers—he is able to describe what enters into his consciousness, whether this be in the form of images or voices.

Watt is a magnificent attempt to embody these inner experiences to which a *higher reality* (neither rational nor merely subjective) corresponds. It is the work of a matter-of-fact, Irish-French intellectual who is as refined in his sensibility as he is uncompromising in his vision; who is as full of creative imagination as he is of cold sobriety; who follows in the footsteps of Watt, that poor, lonely soul, in misery as he first sets out on his life journey on earth, then in qualified, temporary contentment as a neophyte in Mr. Knott's house and garden. Traveling from an unspecific "here" to an "elsewhere" and back again, Watt learns of the tragicomic nature of existence

188. Pp. 71, 74–75. See also n. 39.

and experiences a "counterworld" with all the appearances of the absurd—a world that appears to be off its hinges—in which he is only a shadow among shadows. There Watt must serve for a time before he can return to the plane of ordinary reality. Beckett thus has gone beyond what was achieved in the stream-of-consciousness novel developed by Henry James, James Joyce, and Virginia Woolf. He has pushed forward into the boundary region between life and death to reach a new dimension, a new horizon of consciousness.

The greatest torture for man is his alienation from his spiritual home, which condemns him to wander aimlessly in the world in search of the reality which is found only in death. Beckett perceived this early in life and endured the tragedy it implies. The "original sin" for which man must atone is that of being born at all. In Beckett's essay on Proust we read, "The tragic figure represents the expiation of original sin, of the original and eternal sin of him and all his 'soci malorum,' the sin of having been born."[189] Beckett's tragic figures live a life of expiation for their original sin, either attempting to make the best of a bad situation or trying to overcome their sad state as rapidly as possible by "practicing death," that is, becoming intimate with death by anticipating its reality in their minds.

In his study on Proust Beckett asks: "But what is attainment? The identification of the subject with the object of his desire. The subject has died—and perhaps many times—on the way."[190] In this essay he also mentions Baudelaire's definition of reality as the conformity between subject and object.

Watt raises questions in our minds which cannot be answered by the techniques of literary criticism alone. Neither is a psychologically oriented interpretation sufficient in itself; it must be supplemented by epistemological and anthropological concepts. Otherwise we wind up stranded on the level of psychological relativism, which would block our effort to do

189. *Proust,* p. 49.
190. Ibid., p. 3. Beckett mentions Baudelaire on p. 57.

justice to the stature of the work. The "madhouse theory" is tempting, but it proves to be merely an evasion of the deeper issues. It can be accepted only with certain reservations.[191]

The physiology of the senses is a discipline developing today as part of a more humanly relevant, medically oriented anthropology; it represents a countermovement to the outdated Darwinian concept of man as descendant of the apes. Recent advances in this field provide a basis for a better understanding of *Watt*. It has been found, for example, that the classic physiology of the senses is based on a philosophical dualism between subject and object and that this has led to unresolvable contradictions.[192]

This concerns the nature of sense experience, which, on the basis of this dualism, must be considered purely subjective. If this were correct, objective natural science or even something as simple as the faithful observation of nature would be impossible. The theory of absolute subject-object dualism, if pursued to its logical end, leads to the subjectivism of all the natural sciences. Even the modern concept of cybernetics fails to overcome this subject-object split, because it does nothing to resolve the division of information into formal and semantic content (Hensel).

According to recent findings, however, the act of perception is *a holistic act,* and therefore the concepts of "subject"

191. This is so regardless of Samuel Beckett's opinion, for in purely formal terms we can speak of a "lunatic" situation, and superficially part III, where Sam is told the entire story by Watt, takes place in a kind of mental institution (see n. 123). Thus Beckett responded to a question on this point on April 12, 1978 as follows: "Only one part is in the asylum (though all told there), the other three in Knott's house." (Here Beckett does not consider that in part I Watt has had to travel to Knott's house and later depart from it in part IV, quite aside from the narrative frame at the beginning and at the end, which takes up a large portion of parts I and IV.) In part III Watt is in a state which can be expressed only by means of an "asylum" image. But this does not mean that we have to take this literally and interpret Watt's narrative as the story of a lunatic.

192. See Hans J. Scheurle, *Überwindung der Subjekt-Objekt-Spaltung in der Sinneslehre* (Stuttgart, 1977), with commentary by H. Hensel.

and "object" are secondary to this act. The duality has existence only *in relation to* the whole and thus has only relative significance in this dynamically changing *intentional* act. The subject as perceptive authority is reintroduced into the theory of sense perception. This has far-reaching effects on the evaluation of what a writer like Beckett *perceives* when he embarks on voyages of discovery into his own inner being.

If we accept, furthermore, that man has not only five outward-directed senses but also several inward-directed ones that respond to bodily states and functions, and if we also accept an expansion of the term "perception" to include the areas of understanding language ("speech sense"), thoughts ("thought sense"), and the recognition of the ego ("ego sense"), then we arrive at a complete "sense organism" which corresponds to the observable anthropological facts.[193] By interpreting sensory activity in this way, we overcome the absoluteness of the separation into two qualitatively incommensurable worlds, the inner world and the outer world; and, although it is not my goal here to ignore the real differences between these two areas of experience, we can conclude that in principle the boundary between them can be crossed by an intentional act. By reintroducing the subject in its meaning for every kind of act of perception, it is again possible to feel that one is a "citizen of both worlds" without being banished to a madhouse, overwhelmed by pseudoscientific arguments. The criteria for truthful reporting of inner experiences—which also implies criteria by which the supraindividual value of a "poetic" (fictional) statement is judged—must perhaps be revised in this light.

Correlated with the act of perception are the terms "sense impression" (stimulus) and "sensory content" (knowledge), which are, respectively, equivalents for something objectively measurable and "merely" subjectively felt; but over and above both stands the concept of intentionality, and it

193. See Steiner, *Menschenwerden, Weltenseele und Weltengeist* (*Gesamtausgabe*, vol. 205).

would be an arbitrary act to restrict the meaning of "sense impression" to that which occurs on the physical, organic plane. "Sense perception involves that which is direct and original. Knowledge through perception bears the character of the directly given, of that which is without antecedent."[194] Natural perception, on all planes of reality or sensation, is conditioned by judgment and prejudice. The less these are allowed to influence the act of perception, the more accurate the observation. This applies to the acts of hearing and seeing as much as it does to perceptions of inner processes. That is, it also applies to that which Sam learns from Watt. Freedom from preconceived notions is just as essential for spiritual perception as the health of the physical sensory apparatus is for organic perception. Here again, the whole complex of issues is beset by the problem of identification and objectification—the problem of perception as experience, its mental and concrete realization, and the possibility of its transmission to others.

Beckett's method, as he describes in his essay on Proust, was the path of internalization and contemplation. At the same time, it should not be overlooked that he transcended the subjective realms of experience conveyed in more comprehensible psychological terms by other authors (including Proust) and actually forged into virgin territory.[195]

194. Scheurle, *Überwindung der Subjekt-Objekt-Spaltung in der Sinneslehre*, p. 16.

195. Novalis (Friedrich von Hardenberg), *Fragmente* (Dresden, 1929), p. 388. Novalis considers "extrasensory" perception possible in principle; that is, he believes in the existence of organs of spiritual perception. In Fragment 1110 he asks if our senses are not "modifications of the mind" and as such could we not "modify and direct them as we please." He considers it "the most arbitrary of preconceptions that man does not have the power to "have awareness beyond the senses," that is, to perceive extrasensorily, which sounds like a contradiction in terms, as long as we hold to a limited definition of the senses. Rudolf Steiner, in *Wie erlangt man Erkenntnisse der höheren Welten* (*Gesamtausgabe*, vol. 10), proceeds from the same idea as Novalis to deal with the problem of spiritual perception (see n. 138).

In his own search for the self,[196] Beckett did not simply set aside his everyday ego and advance to the existential thresholds of birth and death. From the experience of the void, which revealed itself to him as the womb of the irrational and became for him a creative source of imagination and intuition, he developed forces which enabled him to see into the world of the unborn and the dead. He also became familiar with the shadow side of his experience, the unavoidable loneliness.[197]

Watt is a milestone on the route to the nonsensory, to "immortality"—to a purely spiritual existence which is the focus of Beckett's expectations, his contemplation, and also his active pursuit. It is no accident that Beckett is in sympathy with Heinrich von Kleist, author of "On the Marionette Theater," an essay which he admires. Kleist's yearning for death is in profound resonance with Beckett's own attitude.[198]

In Beckett's need for quiet and solitude there is a suggestion of his attitude toward death, his desire for the "end of observation," for despite Beckett's reservations, Berkeley's dictum "esse est percipi" fully represents his concept of existence as a process of perception.[199]

Nevertheless, Beckett's own works—including those after *Watt* and the trilogy—attest that death does not necessarily mean the end of self-awareness. We are reminded here of *Play*, *That Time*, and other meditations on the next life. In *Play*, three "heads," staring fixedly forward from funeral urns, re-

196. "The Search for the Self" is the title of Esslin's chapter on Beckett in *The Theatre of the Absurd*.

197. In *Endgame* Beckett has Hamm say, "Infinite emptiness will be all around you, all the resurrected dead of all the ages wouldn't fill it, and there you'll be like a little bit of grit in the middle of the steppe" (p. 36).

198. On the memorial for Kleist at the Wannsee in Berlin, where he took his life on November 21, 1811, there is a quotation from his play, *Prinz von Homburg*: "O immortality—now you are completely mine." This line was cited by Beckett during a conversation in Berlin on February 22, 1975, when the topic turned to Kleist. See also Knowlson and Pilling, "Beckett and Kleist's Essay 'On the Marionette Theatre,' " in *Frescoes of the Skull*, p. 277.

199. See Beckett, *Film*, p. 11.

flect upon their past lives in which destiny had linked them together in a love triangle. In *That Time*, a white-haired old man is confronted by the voices of his own past. Beckett has obviously had a yearning for the solitude of death from early childhood; it has accompanied him throughout his life and has often been interpreted as "depression."[200]

Beckett has always avoided questions on the "meaning" of his works, occasionally with the remark that he is not a philosopher.[201] When he says that he is not a philosopher, we must take this with a grain of salt, for it appears more likely to me that Beckett simply does not expect philosophy to give him satisfactory answers to the existential problems that cause him so much pain. Moreover, the point of art is to make something perceivable to the senses—to make it audible, visible, and so forth. For this reason many artists live in a state of intense sensory activity. It is no different in Beckett's case, and this is the basis of his remark, "Je ne suis que sensibilité."[202]

In relation to *Watt*, the problem is to show where Beckett's intentionality in the act of perception is being directed.

200. Beckett's relationship to stones, which he has called "almost a love relationship," was associated by Beckett himself with death (conversation of September 9, 1967). As a child he frequently picked up stones from the beach and carried them home, where he built nests for them and put them in trees to protect them from the waves and other dangers. On the same occasion, Beckett mentioned Sigmund Freud, who had once written that man carried with him a kind of congenital yearning for the mineral kingdom. This remark followed a discussion of the phenomenon of death, of "dying off," of "petrifying," after I had spoken of "sclerotic traits" in the figure of Krapp. He had me describe these traits to him in detail. Beckett then pointed out that Malone also carried stones around with him, playing "stone games" with them. His remark that there are probably people who are not happy until they have become old enough to have died to a certain extent appeared to me at the time to have a biographical reference.

201. To a question of this nature on April 12, 1969, he thought for a moment, but then said, shrugging his shoulders, "No, it's no good." Then he added that he can form no judgment of his own work or of its meaning (see n. 183).

202. See n. 59.

It is certain that it is not being directed to the perception of the external world. Beckett's gaze is directed entirely within, toward the depths of his being. He did not stop at the stage of subjective self-analysis or self-perception, but transcended the normal horizon of consciousness. In the process he was forced to jettison his private world of ideas and the system of rational thought connected with it. He did not set out in search of things past as Proust did, but rather, in a certain sense, annulled the temporal aspect of existence. He crossed the threshold in his consciousness. He experienced that when this zero point is passed, the world of the mind undergoes a reversal. It was hard to express this in literary images because of the difficulty of keeping them properly organized, but with enormous effort, in a tour de force, he attempted to capture his experiences in words. In addition to seeing images, which still depend heavily on previous experience, he began to hear "voices" speaking to him—Watt's voice.

Watt is obviously not entirely free of subjective elements. It is nevertheless not "mere invention." *Watt* is a record of actual inner events. The visual motifs, the words, the rhythms of the language, and the overall composition are subordinated to this spiritual reality. They are only the means to an end, not the end itself, because their only function is to depict a new plane of reality. Here is the secret of this text. In spite of the difficulty of comprehending it, this is the source of the fascination perceived by everyone who makes a serious attempt to understand *Watt*.

Concluding Remarks

Beckett describes a multidimensional reality in *Watt*, and he has done this with his customary precision. In order to describe a realm of experience which until *Watt* had not been presented in contemporary literature in this form, it was necessary for Beckett to find new forms of expression. The unusual means he found and the experiences presented through them have induced critics to agree that the novel is basically a description of life in a mental institution. In my view, the author Beckett traces Watt's destiny through the stages of birth and death: the entry onto the stage of life, the train journey, the path to Mr. Knott's house, the first crossing of the threshold, the incidents in various regions of the house and garden, and the second crossing of the threshold. The question of reincarnation, in addition to many others, is raised.

No further information can be obtained from Beckett, who has simply described what he experienced. Beckett will not comment beyond the text itself, which aptly formulates these questions of birth and death.

Embodied in the abstruse transformations of consciousness resulting from passage through the various levels of reality—i.e., on entering Mr. Knott's house and leaving it again—is the "esoteric" content of this work, a content which we have approached by interpretive means.

The study presented here arose from an anthropological interest. My approach was phenomenological; that is, the text was studied in terms of its content and its compositional and formal characteristics. The purpose of this analysis was to uncover the gnosiological aspect which we anticipated finding in *Watt*. The figure of Watt is a personified question directed at the spiritual nature of man. The novel *Watt* is a literary formulation of this question and a description of the journey traveled by the human spirit through various levels of awareness.

The phenomenological method applied in this study was suitable not only for illuminating the psychological problems that *Watt* asks the reader to solve, but also for creating an understanding of how Beckett, as the author of a fictional text, could transcend the subjective world of perception and experience and arrive at universally valid spiritual insights in the first place.

Beckett increases our grasp of what life in the body and in certain regions of the spiritual world is like, in that he makes it possible for us to re-create in our own minds Watt's passage through the ordeal of birth and death. This process, embodied in the vicissitudes of Watt's life, has been called the underlying gnosiological aspect of the novel *Watt*.

Bibliography of
Literature Cited

Acheson, James. "Murphy's Metaphysics." *Journal of Beckett Studies* 5 (1979):9–23.
Alvarez, Alfred. *Beckett.* London, 1978.
Anderegg, Johannes. *Literaturwissenschaftliche Stiltheorie.* Göttingen, 1977.

Bair, Deirdre. *Samuel Beckett: A Biography.* New York and London, 1978.
Beckett, Samuel. *Company.* New York, 1980.
――――. "Dante . . . Bruno. Vico . . . Joyce." In *Our Exagmination Round His Factification for Incamination of Work in Progress,* pp. 3–22. Paris, 1929.
――――. *Endgame: A Play in One Act.* New York, 1958. Reprinted in *The Collected Works of Samuel Beckett.* New York, 1970.
――――. *Film.* New York, 1969.
――――. *Mercier and Camier.* London, 1974; New York, 1975.
――――. *More Pricks Than Kicks.* London, 1970.
――――. *Murphy.* New York, 1957.
――――. *No's Knife.* London, 1967.
――――. *Proust.* New York, [1957]. First published London, 1931.
――――. *Rockaby.* New York, 1981.
――――. *Stories and Texts for Nothing.* New York, 1967.
――――. *Waiting for Godot.* New York, 1954.
――――. *Watt.* London: John Calder, 1963.
――――. *Watt.* New York: Grove Press, 1959.
――――. *Watt.* Paris: Edition de Minuit, 1968.
Beckett, Samuel, and George Duthuit. *Bram van Velde.* London: Calder and Boyars, 1965.

Beckett at 60: A Festschrift. London, 1967.

Bernal, Olga. "Das Dilemma der Repräsentation." In *Materialien zu Samuel Becketts Romanen*, edited by Hartmut Engelhardt and Dieter Mettler. Frankfurt am Main, 1976.

――――― . *Langage et fiction dans le roman de Beckett*. Paris, 1969.

Birkenhauer, Klaus. *Beckett*. Reinbek bei Hamburg, 1971.

Bock, Emil. *Wiederholte Erdenleben: Die Wiederverkörperungsidee in der deutschen Geistesgeschichte*. Stuttgart, 1932 and 1952.

Bonnefoy, Claude. *Entretiens avec Eugène Ionesco*. Paris, 1966.

Breuer, Horst. *Samuel Beckett*. Munich, 1972.

Breuer, Rolf. *Die Kunst der Paradoxie*. Munich, 1976.

Brooks, Curtis M. "The Mystic Patterns in *Waiting for Godot*." *Modern Drama* 9 (1966):292–99.

Bryer, Jackson R. "Samuel Beckett: A Checklist of Criticism." In *Samuel Beckett Now: Critical Approaches to His Novels, Poetry, and Plays*, edited by Melvin J. Friedman, pp. 219–59. Chicago, 1970.

Büttner, Gottfried. *Absurdes Theater und Bewusstseinswandel*. Berlin, 1968.

Büttner, Marie Renate. "*Watt* von Samuel Beckett." *Die Christengemeinschaft* 50 (1978):63–65.

Chalker, John. "The Satiric Shape of *Watt*." In *Beckett the Shape Changer*, edited by Katherine Worth, pp. 21–37. London, 1975.

Coe, Richard N. *Beckett*. Edinburgh and London, 1964 and 1968.

Cohn, Ruby, ed. *Casebook on "Waiting for Godot"*. New York, 1967.

――――― . "Philosophical Fragments in the Works of Samuel Beckett." *Criticism: A Quarterly for Literature and the Arts* 6 (1964):33–43. Reprinted in *Samuel Beckett: A Collection of Critical Essays*, edited by Martin Esslin, pp. 169ff.

――――― . *Samuel Beckett: The Comic Gamut*. New Brunswick, N.J., 1962.

――――― . "*Watt* in the Light of *The Castle*." *Comparative Literature* 13 (1961):154–66.

Cousineau, Thomas J. "*Watt*: Language as Interdiction and Consolation." *Journal of Beckett Studies*, no. 4 (1979), pp. 1–13.

d'Aubarède, Gabriele. "En attendant . . . Beckett." *Nouvelles Litteraires*, February 16, 1961. Translation, "Waiting for Beckett," in *Trace*, no. 42 (1961).

DiPierro, J. C. *Structures in Beckett's "Watt."* York, S.C.: French Literature Publications, 1981. I have included this monograph on *Watt* but was unable to discuss it because it was published simultaneously with my own.

Dreysse, Ursula. *Realität als Aufgabe. Eine Untersuchung über Aufbaugesetze und Gehalt des Romanwerks von Samuel Beckett.* Frankfurter Beiträge zur Anglistik und Amerikanistik 5. Bad Homburg v.d.H., Berlin, Zürich, 1970.

Driver, Tom F. "Beckett by the Madeleine." *Columbia Forum* 4 (1961):21–25.

Duckworth, Colin. *Angels of Darkness.* London, 1972.

Durozoi, Gerard. *Beckett.* Paris and Montreal, 1972.

Engelhardt, Hartmut, and Dieter Mettler, eds. *Materialien zu Samuel Becketts Romanen.* Frankfurt am Main, 1976.

Esslin, Martin, ed. *Samuel Beckett: A Collection of Critical Essays.* Englewood Cliffs, N.J., 1965.

———. *The Theatre of the Absurd.* 2d rev. ed. Garden City, N.Y., 1969.

Federman, Raymond. *Journey to Chaos: Samuel Beckett's Early Fiction.* Berkeley and Los Angeles, 1965.

Federman, Raymond, and John Fletcher. *Samuel Beckett: His Works and His Critics.* Berkeley and Los Angeles, 1970.

Fletcher, John. *The Novels of Samuel Beckett.* London, 1964 and 1970.

———. *Samuel Beckett's Art.* London, 1967.

Francis, D. *Samuel Beckett.* London, 1971.

Friedman, Melvin J. "The Novels of Samuel Beckett: An Amalgam of Joyce and Proust." *Comparative Literature* 12 (1960):47–58.

———. *Samuel Beckett Now: Critical Approaches to His Novels, Poetry, and Plays.* Chicago, 1970.

Gessner, Niklaus. "Die Unzulänglichkeit der Sprache: Eine Untersuchung über Formzerfall und Beziehungslosigkeit bei Beckett." Dissertation, Zürich, 1957.

Gölter, Waltraud. *Entfremdung als Konstituens bürgerlicher Literatur, dargestelltl am Beispiel Samuel Becketts.* Studia Romanica 27. Heidelberg, 1976.

Greenberg, Alvin. "The Death of the Psyche: A Way to the Self in the Contemporary Novel." *Criticism* 8 (1966):1–18.

Guggenheim, Margaret. *Confessions of an Art Addict.* New York, 1960.

Harvey, Lawrence E. *Samuel Beckett: Poet and Critic.* Princeton, 1970.

———. "Samuel Beckett—initiation du poète." In *Samuel Beckett— Configuration critique,* edited by Melvin J. Friedman, pp. 153–68. Revues des Lettres moderne 100. Paris, 1964.

Hemleben, Johannes. *Jenseits.* Reinbek bei Hamburg, 1975.

Hensel, G. *Beckett.* Velber, 1968.

Hensel, H. Commentary in *Überwindung der Subjekt-Objekt-Spaltung in der Sinneslehre,* by Hans J. Scheurle. Stuttgart, 1977.

Hesla, David H. "The Defeat of the Proto-Zetetic: Watt." Chap. 3 in his *The Shape of Chaos: An Interpretation of the Art of Samuel Beckett,* pp. 59–85. Minneapolis, 1971.

———. "The Shape of Chaos: A Reading of Beckett's *Watt.*" *Critique* 6 (Minneapolis, 1963):85–105.

Hobson, H. "The First Night of *Waiting for Godot.*" In *Beckett at 60: A Festschrift.* London, 1967.

Hoefer, Jacqueline. "*Watt.*" *Perspective* 11 (1959):166–82. Reprinted in *Samuel Beckett: A Collection of Critical Essays,* edited by Martin Esslin, pp. 62–76. Englewood Cliffs, N.J., 1965.

Hutchinson, M. "All the Livelong Way." In *Beckett at 60: A Festschrift,* pp. 93ff. London, 1967.

Ionesco, Eugène. *Fragments of a Journal.* Translated by Jean Stewart. New York, 1968.

Iser, Wolfgang. *The Act of Reading: A Theory of Aesthetic Response.* Baltimore and London, 1978.

———. *Die Artistik des Misslingens.* Heidelberg, 1979.

———. *The Implicit Reader.* Baltimore and London, 1974.

———. "The Pattern of Negativity in Beckett's Prose." *The Georgia Review* 29 (1975):706–19.

———. "Samuel Becketts dramatische Sprache." *Germanisch-romanische Montasschrift* 11 (1961):451–67.

Jacobsen, Josephine, and William Mueller. *The Testament of Samuel Beckett.* London, 1966.

Janvier, Ludovic. "Les difficultés d'un séjour." *Critique* 263 (Paris, 1969):312–23.

Josipovici, Gabriel, ed. *The Modern English Novel.* London, 1976. See especially "The Fictional Topography of Samuel Beckett," by Robin Lee, pp. 206–24.

Kenner, Hugh. "Der Bereich des Rationalen." In *Materialien zu Samuel Becketts Romanen,* edited by Hartmut Engelhardt and Dieter Mettler, pp. 258ff. Frankfurt am Main, 1976.

Kesting, Marianne. "Das Romanwerk Samuel Becketts." In her *Vermessung des Labyrinths: Studien zur moderne Ästhetik.* Frankfurt am Main, 1965.

Knowlson, James. *Samuel Beckett: A Catalogue.* London, 1971.

Knowlson, James, and John Pilling, eds. *Frescoes of the Skull: The Later Prose and Drama of Samuel Beckett.* London, 1979.

Koestler, Arthur. *The Act of Creation.* London, 1964.

Lee, Robin. "The Fictional Topography of Samuel Beckett." In *The Modern English Novel,* edited by Gabriel Josipovici, pp. 206–24. London, 1976.

Lessing, Gotthold Ephraim. "Eine Duplik." In *Lessing Werke.* Schriften II, vol. 3. Frankfurt am Main, 1967.

_____ . *Zwei Briefe Lessings über den Tod Eva Königs.* Facsimile. Wolfenbüttel: Herzog August Bibliothek, n.d.

Leventhal, A. J. "The Beckett Hero." *Critique: Studies in Modern Fiction* 6 (1964/65):18–35. Reprinted in *Samuel Beckett: A Collection of Critical Essays,* edited by Martin Esslin, pp. 37–51. Englewood Cliffs, N.J., 1965.

Levy, Eric P. *Beckett and the Voice of Species: A Study of the Prose Fiction.* Totowa, N.J., and Dublin, 1980.

Maierhöfer, Fränzi. *Endspiel.* Munich, 1977.

_____ . *Samuel Beckett: Warten auf Godot.* Munich, 1973.

Martel, François. "Jeux formels dans *Watt*." *Poétique* 10 (1972):153–75.

Mayer, Hans, and Uwe Johnson, eds. *Das Werk von Samuel Beckett: Berliner Colloquium.* Frankfurt am Main, 1975.

Mayoux, Jean-Jacques. *Über Beckett.* Frankfurt am Main, 1966.

Mears, Russell. "Beckett, Sarraute, and the Perceptual Experience of Schizophrenia." *Psychiatry,* no. 36 (1973), pp. 61–69.

Monteith, Charles. "A Personal Note." In *Beckett at 60: A Festschrift.* London, 1967.

Mood, John J. " 'The Personal System'—Samuel Beckett's *Watt*." *PMLA* 86 (1971):255–65.

Moody, Raymond A. *Leben nach dem Tod.* Reinbek bei Hamburg, 1977.

Moorjani, Angela B. "Narrative Game Strategies in Beckett's *Watt*." *L'Esprit créateur* 17 (1977):235–44.

Morse, J. Mitchell. "The Contemplative Life According to Samuel Beckett." *Hudson Review* 15 (1962/63):512–24.

Pilling, John. *Samuel Beckett*. London and Boston, 1976.

Rabinovitz, Rubin. "*Molloy* and the Archetypal Traveller." *Journal of Beckett Studies*, no. 5 (1979), pp. 25–44.

Reichel, Edward. "Der Roman und das Geschichtenerzählen." *Deutsche Vierteljahrsschrift für Literaturwissenschaft und Geistesgeschichte* [*DVJS*] 52 (1978):296–345.

Rohmann, Gerd, ed. *Laurence Sterne*. Darmstadt, 1980.

Rosen, Steven J. *Samuel Beckett and the Pessimistic Tradition*. New Brunswick, N.J., 1976.

Rusterholz, P. "Semiotik und Hermeneutik." *Prisma*, no. 23 (1980), pp. 10–15.

Scheurle, Hans J. *Überwindung der Subjekt-Objekt-Spaltung in der Sinneslehre*. Stuttgart, 1977.

Schneider, Alan. "Waiting for Beckett." *Chelsea Review*, no. 2 (1958), pp. 3–20. Reprinted in *Beckett at 60: A Festschrift*, pp. 34ff. London, 1967.

Schoell, Konrad. "The Chain and the Circle: A Structural Comparison of *Waiting for Godot* and *Endgame*." *Modern Drama* 11 (1968):48–53.

——— . *Das Theater Samuel Becketts*. Munich, 1967.

Schröder, Ernst. "Proben mit Beckett." *Frankfurter Allgemeine Zeitung*, November 17, 1967.

Seaver, Richard W., ed. *I can't go on, I'll go on: A Selection from Samuel Beckett's Work*. New York, 1976.

Senneff, Susan Field. "Song and Music in Samuel Beckett's *Watt*." *Modern Fiction Studies* 10 (1964):137–49.

Smuda, Manfred. *Becketts Prosa als Metasprache*. Munich, 1970.

Stanzel, Frank K. "Towards a Grammar of Fiction." *Novel* 11 (1978):247–64.

Steiner, Rudolf. *Rudolf Steiner Gesamtausgabe*. Vols. 4, 9, 13, 17, 29, 109, 111, 145, 206, 282, and 350. Dornach bei Basel.

Swanson, Eleanor. "Samuel Beckett's *Watt*: A Coming and A Going." *Modern Fiction Studies* 17 (1971):264–68.

Tophoven, Elmar. "En traduisant Beckett." In *Das Werk Samuel Beck-etts: Berliner Colloquium,* edited by Hans Mayer and Uwe John-son, pp. 159ff. Frankfurt am Main, 1975.

Trivisonno, Ann M. "Meaning and Function of the Quest in Beck-ett's *Watt.*" *Critique* 12 (Minneapolis, 1969):28–38.

Warhaft, Sidney. "Threne and Theme in *Watt.*" *Wisconsin Studies in Contemporary Literature* 4 (1963):261–78.

Wasserman, Jerry. "Watt's World of Words." In *Twentieth-Century Poetry, Fiction, Theory,* edited by Harry R. Garvin, pp. 123–38. Lewisburgh, Pa., and London, 1977.

Webb, Eugene. *Samuel Beckett: A Study of His Novels.* London, 1970.

Wellek, René, and Austin Warren. *Theory of Literature.* 3d ed. New York, 1956.

Wiedemann, G. *Gedanken über die Unsterblichkeit als Wiederholung des Erdenlebens.* Stuttgart, 1961.

Winston, Mathew. "*Watt's* First Footnote." *Journal of Modern Literature* 6 (1977):69–82. Beckett issue.

Worth, Katherine, ed. *Beckett the Shape Changer.* London, 1975.

About the Author

Gottfried Büttner was born on March 13, 1926, in Dresden, Germany. After completing his secondary schooling in his native town in 1947, he studied medicine at the Universities of Göttingen and Tübingen in West Germany. He received his first degree (M.D.) in 1953 and has been a practicing physician of general medicine ever since.

Dr. Büttner has published several books on medical and literary themes. In 1978 he became a part-time lecturer at the University of Hessen in Kassel. The psychology of literature being his main interest, he has taught on such topics as the theater of the absurd and James Joyce. In 1980 he received his second degree (Ph.D).

Since 1952 he has been married to Marie Renate Büttner, née Neindorf, also a physician.